Paper Quilling

for the first time®

Paper Quilling

for the first time®

Alli Bartkowski

Sterling Publishing Co., Inc. New York

A Sterling/Chapelle Book

Chapelle, Ltd.,
  P.O. Box 9252, Ogden, UT 84409
  (801) 621-2777 • (801) 621-2788 Fax
  e-mail: chapelle@chapelleltd.com
  Web site: www.chapelleltd.com

Library of Congress Cataloging-in-Publication Data

Bartkowski, Alli.
  Paper quilling for the first time / Alli Bartkowski.
    p. cm.
  Includes index.
  ISBN-13: 978-1-4027-2216-5
  ISBN-10: 1-4027-2216-8
1. Paper quillwork. I. Title.
TT870.B242 2006
745.54--dc22   2005027791

10 9 8 7 6 5 4 3 2 1
Published by Sterling Publishing Co., Inc.
387 Park Avenue South, New York, NY 10016
©2006 by Alli Bartkowski
Distributed in Canada by Sterling Publishing
⅟ Canadian Manda Group, 165 Dufferin Street
Toronto, Ontario, Canada M6K 3H6
Distributed in the United Kingdom by GMC Distribution Services, Castle Place, 166 High Street, Lewes, East Sussex, England BN7 1XU
Distributed in Australia by Capricorn Link (Australia) Pty. Ltd.
P.O. Box 704, Windsor, NSW 2756, Australia
Printed and Bound in China
All Rights Reserved

Sterling ISBN-13: 978-1-4027-2216-5
          ISBN-10: 1-4027-2216-8
  For information about custom editions, special sales, premium and corporate purchases, please contact Sterling Sales Department at 800-805-5489 or specialsales@sterlingpub.

Table of Contents

Introduction

Welcome to the amazing art of quilling, or paper filigree! It is definitely an art form that excites and impresses you from the very first quilled piece. At first glance, most people say, "What is it?", "How did you do that?", or "Is that really paper?" But once they try rolling and shaping their first quilled piece, their mood changes to excitement and they'll say, "Wow, I can't believe how simple it is!" and ask, "What else can I make with rolled paper strips?" Then before they realize it, they're hooked.

The art of quilling dates as far back as the 16th and 17th centuries when the French and Italian nuns and monks would decorate reliquaries, holy pictures, and frames with quilled pieces. The strips of paper were wrapped and rolled around a feather quill, hence the name "quilling." Silver and gold gilded-edge papers from books were trimmed off, rolled, and attached to their artwork to imitate the look of metal filigree. This clever technique was much more affordable, versatile, and easier to do than actual metalwork. It eventually spread to England where many "ladies of leisure" and proper young ladies would be taught this decorative and elegant paper art. Like needlework, they used their pastime to quill on tea caddies, jewelry boxes, screens, handbags, and furniture. It was brought to the American colonies where the art continued to be taught and placed on pictures, sconces, and wooden boxes.

Today, quilling complements very nicely with scrapbooking, card making, framing, and other well-made crafts because, as in any handmade treasure, it's done with patience, pride, and love. From my experience, a handmade quilled card always touches the heart of the recipient and a framed, quilled wedding invitation will be cherished by the bride and groom for a lifetime.

Perhaps the undeniable appeal for this art may be the fascination people have with paper. How often do you take a paper brochure, map, or ticket and roll it until it's beyond recognition? Then, there is the relaxing, or "calming of the nerves," effect when paper is worked between the fingers. It could also be the satisfied feeling and amazement when you see a finished quilled project that looks incredibly intricate to create when it actually was very simple to produce. Whatever the case, you will not be disappointed with the possibilities that this art presents to you. It's an art form that many past generations have enjoyed, treasured, and preserved. So, get ready to discover the amazing art of quilling and find your creative quilling side.

See Butterfly Paperweight on pages 53–56.

How to Use this Book

When I started to write *Quillling for the first time*®, I was excited at the opportunity of what I could include. The first thing I said was that this book is going to be filled with pictures to describe every technique in quilling. Often I've found that written text is not enough to describe a certain quilling technique and wished there was a way to show it through pictures. This book will hopefully serve that purpose, not only for beginners, but for any quiller who wants to see more techniques than just rolling paper strips.

Section 1: Getting Started will familiarize you with the various quilling tools and materials you will need to get started. I've also included some wonderful tools that will help make cards and scrapbook pages a little easier.

Section 2: The Basics has fourteen basic techniques in quilling that are my favorite and that I found to be the most popular in the quilling world. For each technique, there is a fun project to help you make a beautifully quilled card or piece about which you will proudly say, "I made it myself!" For beginner quillers, I recommend looking over the first four techniques carefully since they are the foundation for quilling. The other techniques are independent from each other and will show how much more you can make with paper strips.

Section 3: Beyond the Basics combines techniques, paper widths, punched papers, and other materials to accent your quilled pieces. The projects are not necessarily more difficult, but they take more time and patience to complete since they include more individual pieces.

Section 4: The Gallery provides some incredible quilled works from experienced quilling artists. You can see the variety of ideas that will hopefully inspire you to discover the versatility and beauty of quilling.

See Hummingbird & Buttercup on pages 63–65.

Section 1: *Getting Started*

Quilling Basics

Quilling originally started with a feather quill, strips of paper and very creative hands. Some traditional quillers enjoy rolling their paper strips with their fingers and fringing papers by hand. However, most of today's quillers love time-saving and ergonomically designed tools to quickly and easily roll their papers. They also enjoy simple and creative designs that can be completed in one sitting, which is perfect for making scrapbook pages, gift tags, and homemade cards.

One of the best things about quilling is that it is inexpensive and very portable. The basic slotted and needle tools range from $3.00 to $5.00. Then you'll need strips of paper to help you get started. A useful and multifunctional tool is a circle template board. It's a great tool to help beginners and experts achieve uniform-sized coils for symmetrical quilled designs, like snowflakes and flowers.

There are many other useful quilling tools and accessories designed to stretch your creativity. Some of them are not needed right away to learn the basics of quilling. But once you fall in love with this paper art and you have tried all of the techniques, you will find the other tools and accessories a wonderful addition to your quilling supply collection.

SUPPLIES & TOOLS

For the most basic quilling project, you will need a few tools and paper strips to learn the fundamentals of quilling. Once you've tried it, you'll be pleasantly amazed how quick and simple it is to learn the basic quilled shapes and scrolls. This section in the book will describe in more detail how to use each of the tools and other supplies.

General Quilling Tools

1. **Slotted tool** is a tool for beginners because the slot at the tip helps with the start of rolling. It leaves a slightly larger center with a small fold at the center of the coil. It is easier to learn to quill with this tool. See page 16 on how to roll paper with the slotted tool.

2. **Needle tool** is the preferred tool by experienced quillers because it leaves a smaller center compared to the slotted tool. It takes a little more patience and practice to learn to roll the paper strip with the needle tool. The metal tip of the needle tool can also be used for scoring papers and piercing holes for a decorative look. See pages 16–17 on how to roll paper with the needle tool.

3. **Fine-tipped tweezers** make a great substitute for fingers. They are helpful for holding, gluing, positioning, and assembling quilled pieces. They are almost essential when working with small pieces, especially with miniatures.

4. **Quilling paper** is readily available in various widths, weights, and colors.

5. **Craft glue** can have a big influence on the look of the finished quilled piece. Use a paper craft glue that dries clear, quickly, and rubs off easily from your fingers and tools. *Note: A good test to see if a glue is too tacky for quilling is to place it on your finger and rub it between your fingers and thumbs. If it easily "balls up" and falls off your fingers, then it's good for quilling.*

6. **Sticky-notepad sheet** is used for holding a puddle of glue.

7. **Circle template board** is used for creating consistent and perfectly proportioned quilled coils and shapes.

8. **Ruler** is used if your circle template board does not have a ruler on it.

9. **Fine-tipped scissors** are for hand-fringing, trimming, and cutting detailed shapes.

10. **Straight pins** are for making off-centered circles and shapes, husking, weaving, and assembling the quilled pieces together. Rustproof pins are recommended if using pins where it may come in contact with glue for a long period of time, such as a plug for the glue bottle.

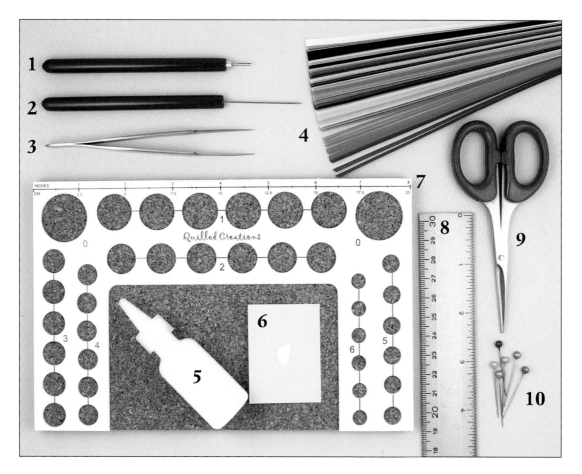

Quilling Papers

Quilling papers come in different widths and lengths. They can range from $1.40 to $5.00 per pack, depending on the number of strips and variety of colors in the pack.

Acid-free

As in scrapbooking and card making, you want your designs and cherished masterpieces to last for generations. It's best to choose and use quilling papers that are free of acid to help protect your photographs and artwork.

Types & Weights

Text-weight paper is the most common and the easiest type with which to quill. It creates beautiful small centers in the coils and it can be pinched easily into various shapes. Professional precision-cut quilling papers produce the best designs because of their clean-cut edges and uniform paper width. When all of the pieces are put together, the design will be even from one shape to the next. Strips of paper can be cut by hand, using scissors, with a small paper cutter, or with a paper shredder; however it may be difficult to keep the assembled pieces all the same height.

Vellums give an interesting translucent effect in your quilling artwork. It can be a little tricky to roll because of its smooth surface. It also will take the glue slightly longer to dry on vellums.

Cardstock can also be used to quill simple designs. It can be rolled by hand or with a tool, but it's more difficult because the fibers can split apart when rolling. Many experienced quillers do not recommend this paper weight because your quilling will not be as detailed and intricate since the coils are thicker and bulkier. The techniques and tools described in this book are designed for text-weight papers.

Widths

The majority of quilling is done with the ⅛" (3mm) width paper. This width is the easiest to learn to roll and it works perfectly with scrapbooking and card making. The wider widths, ¼" (6mm) and ⅜" (9mm), are useful for making fringed flowers, folded roses, and paper sculpting. The narrow width ¹⁄₁₆" (1.5mm) is often used for miniatures or low-profile quilled designs. It isn't used that often, but a simple way to make ¹⁄₁₆"-wide paper strips is to cut a ⅛"-wide paper in half lengthwise.

Graduated & Dark-center Graduated Color

Graduated-color quilling papers offer a unique look to quilled designs. The graduated-color papers start as a solid color and gradually fade to white. The dark-centered graduated papers are the same as the graduated; but they start with white at one edge, fade to the solid color in the center, then gradually fade back to white. The subtle shift in the colors results in eye-catching dimensional shapes that really jump out against a dark background.

Metallic & Gilded Edge

Metallic quilling paper has a gold or silver finish on one side of the paper. It's also known as "quill trim." It should be rolled with the metallic finish showing on the outside. Gilded-edge papers are quilling papers with a metallic or pearlized finish on the edges of the paper strips. When it's rolled and shaped, the gilded edges bring out the beauty of the quilled coils. This effect also can be produced by applying watercolor metallic paints to the top of the quilled pieces.

Two-tone

Two-tone colored quilling papers offer another unique look to quilled designs. These papers are a solid color on one side and the other side is a lighter shade of that same color. As you quill with this paper, you will notice the two tones of the paper throughout each spiral. The beauty of this paper is brought out in the "husking" technique.

The daisy on the above card was created from graduated bright green paper. See Gerbera Daisy Card on pages 45–49.

OTHER TOOLS USED FOR QUILLING

After learning the simple basics in quilling, you will love these other tools and supplies that make quilling faster and easier to do.

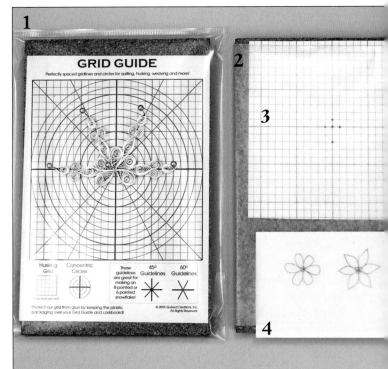

1. **Corkboard** is used for quilling large patterns. Typically, larger patterns will have many small pieces that are held together by pins and glued together. *Note: The board can be made with corkboard, foam-core board, or corrugated cardboard.*

2. **Waxed paper or transparent plastic bag** is used to prevent glue from sticking to the pattern.

3. **Grid or graph paper** is used for husking, weaving, and other quilling techniques. Concentric circles and marked angles of 45 or 60 degrees are helpful for making symmetrical designs such as snowflakes.

4. **Tracing paper** is used for duplicating patterns and designs to protect the original design.

5. **Fringer** is used for fringing paper strips. It cuts and automatically advances wider-width paper strips. This tool is definitely a great time-saver and easy on the hands when making many fringed flowers.

6. **Crimper** (large or small) is used for creating a zigzag look on the paper.

7. **Paper punches** are used for creating basic shapes. A punched flower or leaf complements nicely with quilling. The heart punch is a quick method for making flower petals.

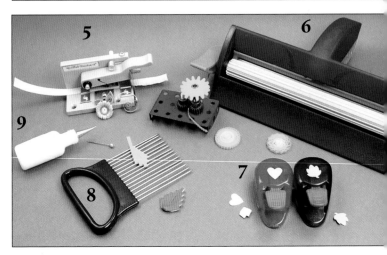

8. **Onion holder or pick comb** is used for looping paper strips described in the combing technique to create interesting petals, leaves and wings.

9. **Ultrafine-tipped glue bottle** is used for quickly dispensing fine lines and drops of glue.

OTHER SUPPLIES TO ACCENT & EMBELLISH QUILLING

1. **Fine-tipped pens & markers** are used for writing, accenting, and embellishing projects.

2. **Chalk palette & applicators** are for creating a soft accent on projects.

3. **Metallics, iridescent & watercolor paints** are for accenting projects and the edges of quilled pieces.

4. **Stamp & ink pad** are for accenting and embellishing projects.

5. **Beads, moveable eyes, rhinestones & sequins** are for adding dimensional embellishments on projects.

6. **Pearls, ribbons & trims** are used for adding dimensional embellishments on projects.

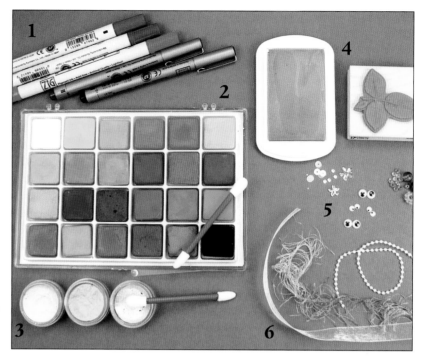

CARD-MAKING & SCRAPBOOKING TOOLS

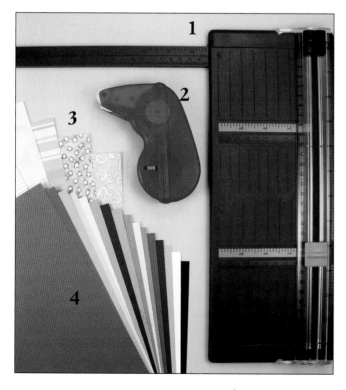

It's extremely helpful to have some basic tools when card making and scrapbooking. Most quilling is done on keepsake items and cherished cards. So these tools will be useful when making projects in this book and for your future projects.

1. **Paper trimmer** is used for trimming paper and cardstock. Most paper trimmers have a cutting blade and a scoring blade. A 12" paper cutter is the recommended size since it will fit the popular size for scrapbook pages.

2. **Tape runner or adhesive tabs** are for dispensing small, precut, double-sided adhesive tabs that allow you to quickly mount paper together. This can be better than wet glues, which may wrinkle or leave "air bubbles" in the paper.

3. **Patterned papers** are used as the background pages or to embellish a background page.

4. **Cardstock** is used for the background page.

ROLLING COILS

To begin rolling paper, practice rolling with 8" paper strips.

Slotted Tool

1. Slide the end of the paper into the slot, from the top.

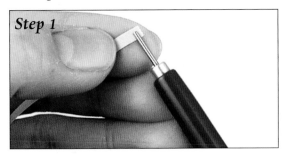

2. Twirl the tool in either direction. Use the tip of your finger to support the coil and your thumb to guide the paper while rolling.

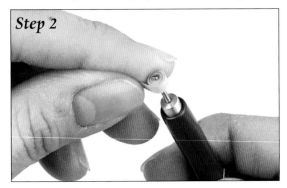

3. When you get to the end of the strip, remove the coil by pushing from behind, or underneath, the coil instead of pulling the coil off from its sides. *Note: This prevents the center of the coil from being pulled out.*

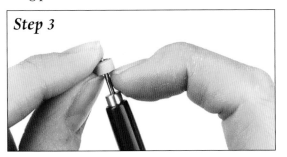

4. Place the coil in the circle template board or on a smooth table surface. Let the coil expand open.

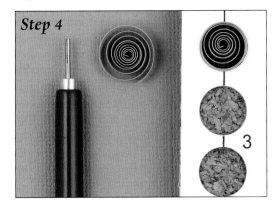

Needle Tool

1. Pull the paper between your forefinger nail and your thumb to curl the paper. *Notes: It's a helpful technique to soften the paper and break the fibers in preparation for rolling.*

You can also moisten the end slightly so that it sticks to the needle when you are ready to roll it.

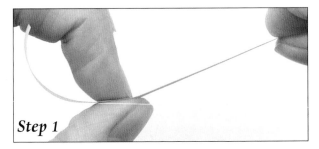

2. Wrap the paper end around the needle tool.

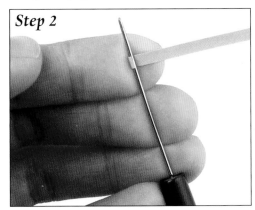

3. Keep the needle tool stationary, then move your thumb and finger in opposite directions to get the roll started. Keep constant light pressure on the coil as you roll so that it does not unravel.

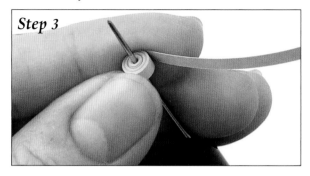

Step 3

4. Slide the coil off the needle tool. Place it in the circle template board or on a smooth table surface. Let the coil expand open.

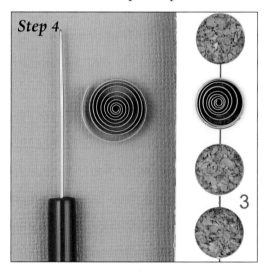

Step 4

ROLLING TECHNIQUES

Every quiller rolls their paper strips slightly differently. We all use different fingertip pressure and tension, creating a variety of coil sizes. Below are some useful tips and techniques to help fix any quilling quirks.

Pulled-out Centers

Instead of pulling, push the coil off the tool to avoid the centers from staying behind on the tool.

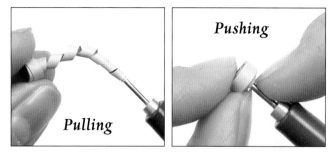

Pushing

Pulling

Pop-ups

Try keeping the paper's edges even as you are rolling the paper strip. This pop-up quilling "quirk" will go away with practice.

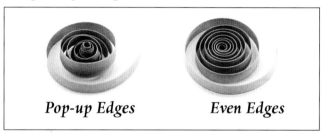

Pop-up Edges   *Even Edges*

Tight Twirler

If your coils aren't expanding, then try relaxing the winding tension, or fingertip pressure, on the roll. Sometimes holding the rolled paper in your hand for too long will prevent the coil from expanding.

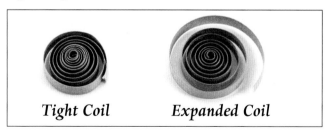

Tight Coil   *Expanded Coil*

Uneven Coils

Using the slotted tool, apply firm, even tension, or fingertip pressure, on the paper strip while rotating the tool.

Using the needle tool, try to use constant fingertip pressure as you are rolling.

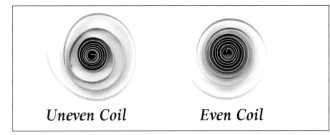

Uneven Coil   *Even Coil*

Uneven Tight Circles

Use less tension, or fingertip pressure, as you roll so that the paper can shift slightly after rolling. Then after the paper's end is glued, place it on a hard surface and use the tool's handle to roll over the top edge, like rolling out a piecrust.

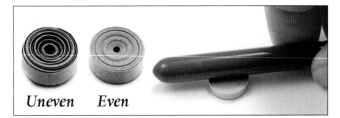

Uneven   *Even*

OTHER QUILLING TECHNIQUES
Tearing Paper Strips

Tearing the paper strip is a favorite technique among quillers because it leaves a feather end. When the paper's end is glued to the coil, the feathered tear is virtually seamless. Conversely, cutting the strip will leave a blunt end that is more visible.

Gluing a Coil

After the coil has been rolled and expanded open, glue the end to the coil, using the following method.

1. Place a puddle of glue on a sticky-notepad sheet.

Step 1

2. Using the needle tool, place a dab of glue at the paper's end.

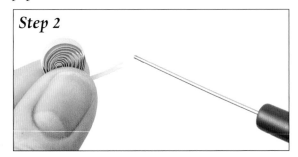

Step 2

3. Use the needle tool to press the glued end flat against the coil.

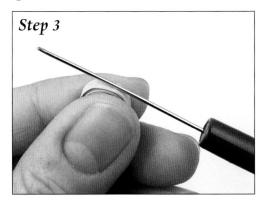

Step 3

Using Patterns

For each project, patterns are provided to help show the actual size of the quilled piece or final design. Since everyone quills with slightly different fingertip pressure, line-drawings are a great reference to make your pieces to scale. The patterns in each project may include the individual quilled shape and/or the assembled finished project. If you would like to use the patterns as a guide, use the following instructions:

1. To protect the original patterns in this book, use a pencil to copy the pattern or patterns onto tracing paper.

2. Roll each piece as instructed. Place the quilled piece on the traced pattern to check the size and placement as shown in 2a.

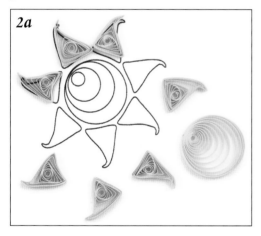

2a

TIP: It is easier to make all of the pieces first and then glue the pieces together or to your background.

Some of the projects will only show a half pattern as shown below. See Scrolled Border Frame on pages 33–34 and Snowflake Ornament on pages 74–76. If the design is symmetrical, copy half of the project pattern, then flip it over and trace the remaining half to make the complete pattern.

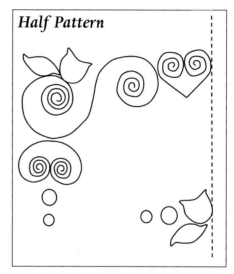

Half Pattern

If the pattern shows eccentric circles or shapes within the design as shown below, this indicates that the coil should be made into an off-centered circle. See Off-Centered Circle Technique on page 29.

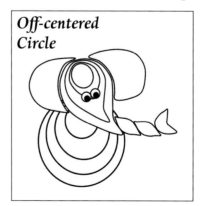

Off-centered Circle

Gluing onto the Background

After quilling all of your pieces, use the following method to glue individual pieces or a small quilled assembly to the background.

1. Place a puddle of glue on a sticky-notepad sheet.

2. Using fine-tipped tweezers, pick up the quilled piece. Hold the piece by the outer coils to get a good grasp on the piece without changing its shape.

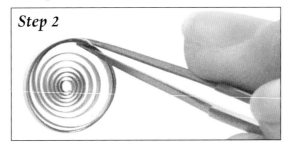

3. Dip the quilled piece into the puddle of glue. If there is too much glue on the strip, then tap the piece on the notepad sheet to remove any excess glue.

4. Place the glued piece on the background.

The quilled pieces featured on this card were glued onto its background, using Steps 1–4, at left and above.

STORING YOUR SUPPLIES & TOOLS

Quilling doesn't take up much space. It's a light-weight and portable craft that can be taken on long road trips or even on vacation. It's best to work on a flat and clean surface like a tabletop, or on a lap-desk if you like to work in front of the television.

Storing Supplies

Group papers together by colors or widths. Store the papers in a plastic container or shoe box for portability. It's an easy and quick way to take papers with you. Another method is to use a metal ring and the hang hole in the packaging to hook the papers together. The best way to keep the papers in good shape and in their original packaging is by making an opening in the bag. Pull out one strip at a time from the inside layer.

Embroidery floss boxes are very effective for separating finished quilled pieces. It's a great way to build up your supply of quilled pieces so they are readily available for use.

Storing Tools

Tools can be stored on your crafting table by pushing them into a Styrofoam® block. It is a convenient holder to keep your tools from rolling away and within reach.

FRAMING QUILLED ARTWORK

Shadowboxes are the best type of frame to display and protect your quilled artwork. These frames have ½"–1" space between the glass and the surface background of your quilled artwork. More stores are carrying shadowbox frames, since memento and keepsake frames are very popular. If you need a customized shadowbox frame or mat, a frame shop is a great resource for ideas and materials.

Another simple way to keep the glass away from your quilled artwork is to make "tight circle" paper spacers. See Tight Circle on page 25. First, choose the paper width based on how far away the glass should be away from the quilled artwork. Roll small tight circles with the paper strips, then glue them around the perimeter of the framed artwork, hidden behind the framework.

PRESERVING QUILLED ARTWORK

Preserving your quilled artwork will ensure that it will last and give it some durability. Many quillers use an acrylic spray sealant to protect their work. Whatever the case may be, practice on a scrap quilled piece first to be certain it is the finish that you prefer.

Section 2: *The Basics*

Method B:
- Using the needle tool, wrap the paper end around the needle and start rolling. Keep constant light pressure on the coil as you roll so that it does not unravel. Once you've rolled to the end, slip it off the needle tool and do not let it expand. Place a dab of glue on the loose end and press it against the tight circle.

2. To even out the edges, place the tight circle on a hard surface and use the handle of the tool to roll across the top of the edges.

Grape Roll

Roll a tight circle from a paper strip. Gently push the center of the tight circle out with your finger or the end of the tool to form a dome. To push

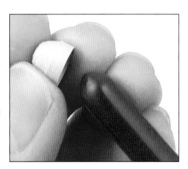

the center out evenly, slightly rotate the tight coil after each push. Place a thin layer of glue on the inner (or outer) surface to preserve the shape. *Note: It may take up to a day for the piece to be "cured" and permanently keep its shape.*

TIP: If you are making multiple grape rolls of the same size, then use a mold (e.g. wooden ball, marble, dome, etc.) to shape each piece.

Cone Roll

Roll a short paper strip into a tight circle, but offset the paper's edge on a slight angle while rolling. Glue the end to the tight circle.

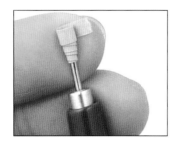

Curving Basic Shapes

Curving the basic quilled shape's point or side can give the piece more character and artistic detail.

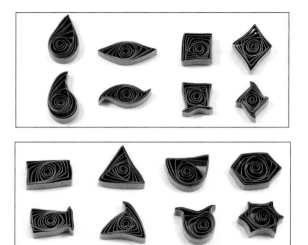

Curving a shape can be done, using one of the following methods:

Method A:
- Using your fingernail, curve the point.

Method B:
- Using the quilling tool, curve the point.

Pinching the basic shapes will allow you to create endless shapes and designs, which is why so many crafters are fascinated by quilling. A helpful method to hide the seam of the paper on your roll is to pinch the point at that seam. Rounding sides inward is also a fun way to change the shape of your quilled piece. Paper is a very forgiving material. So reshape and repinch points whenever necessary to make the right shape.

Flower Card

Here's How:

Finished size: 5" square

1. Cut 5" x 10" card base from white cardstock. Score and fold in half to the finished size.

2. Cut two 1½" squares from pink cardstock and fuchsia cardstock.

3. Cut four burgundy squares that are slightly smaller than the pink and fuchsia squares.

4. Center and mount the burgundy squares to the pink and fuchsia squares with adhesive tabs.

5. **Quilling Instructions**
   For **Teardrop Flower**:
   - Roll six 6" pink paper strips into teardrops. Glue the points together to form a six-petal flower. Roll a 4" white paper strip into a tight circle. Glue to the flower's center as shown in 5a.

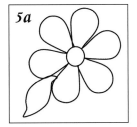

For **Marquise Flower**:
- Roll six 6" pink paper strips into marquises. Glue the points together to form a six-petal flower. Make three 2" white paper strips into tight circles. Glue to the flower's center as shown in 5b.

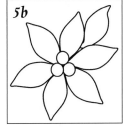

For **Curved Teardrop Flower**:
- Roll five 6" pink paper strips into curved teardrops. Glue rounded portion of the teardrops together, form-ing a five-petal flower. Roll a 2" white paper strip into loose circle. Glue to flower's center as shown in 5c.

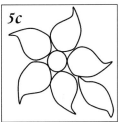

For **Grape-roll Flower**:
- Roll five 16" fuchsia paper strips into grape rolls. Pinch a point on the wider portion of the roll to form a teardrop. Glue the points together to form a five-petal flower. Roll a 2" white paper strip into a cone roll. Glue to flower's center as shown in 5d.

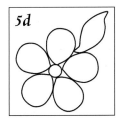

For **Leaves**:
- Roll four 6" green paper strips into curved marquises. Glue a single green leaf to each flower.

6. Using the tweezers, pick up each flower and glue it to each square. Center and mount the squares with flowers to the card base with adhesive tabs.

TIP: To make uniform petals, use a circle template board.

2 Technique

How do I make off-centered or eccentric circles?

What you need to get started:

- General Quilling Tools on pages 10–11

- ⅛"-wide quilling papers: two shades of yellow

- Adhesive tabs

- Cardstock:
  black
  dark green
  moss green

- Paper trimmer with cutting and scoring blades

- Yellow patterned papers

Off-centered or eccentric circles are made from basic loose circles. It is a great technique to add visual perspective to your large quilled circles. A helpful hint: when you are ready to glue it to the background, place the glued side face down so that it does not show in your final quilled artwork.

OFF-CENTERED CIRCLE TECHNIQUE

1. Roll a strip of paper and place it in the circle template board. Let it expand and unroll into the size of the circle opening. Add a dab of glue behind the paper's end to form a loose circle.

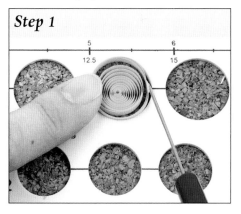

Step 1

2. With a straight pin, pull the center off to the side and push the pin into the board. Then spread a small amount of glue at the top edges of the paper strip near the pin. When the glue has dried, twist to release any dried glue stuck to the pin, then remove the pin.

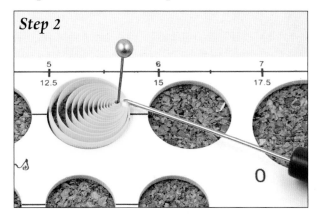

Step 2

TIPS: Use tweezers to arrange and even out your coils before gluing the off-centered center.

To make off-centered circles without a circle template board, use a corkboard and place pins around the loose circle to hold it in place, then use a pin to pull the center off to one side and pin it down into the board.

Sunshine Card

Here's How:

Finished size: 5½" x 4"

1. Cut a 5½" x 8" card base from the moss green cardstock. Score and fold in half to the finished size. Cut a 5¼" x 3¾" rectangle from the dark green cardstock and mount to the card base with adhesive tabs.

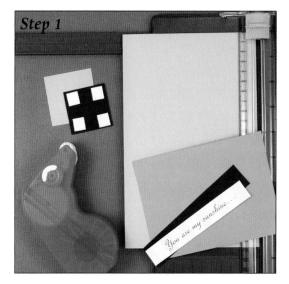

Step 1

2. Cut a 2" square from the moss green cardstock. Cut a 1¼" square from black cardstock. Center and mount onto the moss green square with adhesive tabs.

3. Print on the yellow patterned paper "You are my sunshine . . ." Trim around saying as desired. Center and mount onto black cardstock. Trim black cardstock as desired.

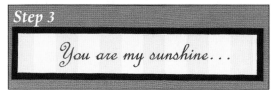

Step 3

You are my sunshine...

4. **Quilling Instructions**

For **Sun**:

- For center, roll a 16" light yellow paper strip into off-centered circle as shown in 4a.

- For rays, roll seven 8" yellow paper strips into triangles with a curved point. Refer to Triangle on page 25.

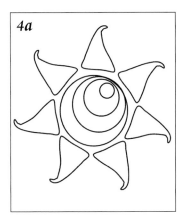

4a

5. Place the sun with the glued side face down in the center of the black square. Arrange the rays around the sun.

Step 5

You are my sunshine . . .

6. Using the tweezers, pick up each piece and glue it to the black square. Mount the square piece with the quilled sun and the "You are my sunshine . . ." piece to the dark green card base with adhesive tabs.

The quilled embellishments on the scrapbook page at right include off-centered circles. The ballerina shoes are off-centered circles made with two paper strips glued together, using the End-to-end Technique on page 36. The off-centered circle in the ballerina dress was pinched and shaped to form the bodice.

How do I make basic quilled scrolls?

Scrolls are made by rolling a strip of paper, but the end is not typically glued to the roll. This is a popular technique for making vines, borders, and alphabet letters. The other scroll techniques described in this section will show how to give your scrolls an artistic and whimsical look.

Technique 3

What you need to get started:

• General Quilling Tools on pages 10–11

• ⅛"-wide quilling papers:
   ivory
   moss green
   pink

• 5" x 7" shadowbox with black mat

• Photograph

31

BASIC SCROLL TECHNIQUES

Loose Scroll

Start rolling the paper strip at one end. Leave the other end loose or straight.

Heart Scroll

Make a fold at the center of the paper strip, then roll each end inward toward the fold. Use a dab of glue to keep the heart scrolls closed.

"C" Scroll

Roll both ends of the paper strip to the center.

"S" Scroll

Roll one end of the paper strip to the center, then turn the strip and roll the other end to the center.

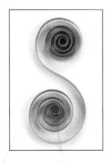

"V" Scroll

Make a fold at the center of the paper strip and roll each end outward.

"Y" Scroll

Make a fold at the center of the paper strip and roll each end outward. Place a dab of glue between the paper strips near the fold.

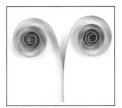

Spiral

Roll a spiral, using one the following methods:

Method A:

- Using the slotted tool, roll the paper strip around the tool. While the coil is on the tool, gently pull the end away from the coil at an angle, unraveling the strip and creating a spiral.

Method B:

- Using the needle tool, place the end of the paper at an angle near the middle of the needle. Roll the paper around the needle so that the spiral rolls up toward the tip of the tool. *Note: Spirals made with the needle tool will be smaller and tighter than the slotted tool.*

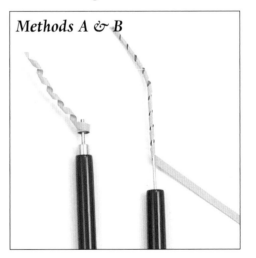

Methods A & B

TIP: After forming the spiral on the tool, tighten it by holding both ends of the spiral and stretching and retwisting it to the desired thickness.

OTHER SCROLL TECHNIQUES

The helpful scroll techniques described below are great for making alphabet letters and beautiful scrolled border designs.

Open Scroll

This is a very simple technique to make the scroll larger with more space between the coils. First unravel part of the scroll, then gently reroll the scroll.

Pinching a Point

Place a small amount of glue at the fold. Pinch the fold closed and hold for a few seconds.

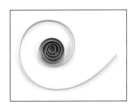

Round Scroll

Pull one end of the paper strip along the needle tool to round or curl end to the desired shape.

Zigzag Scroll

Make two opposing folds near the center of the paper strip. Make two more opposing folds to form the zigzag. Place glue between the folds and press the strips together. Roll the ends of the paper stirp.

Scrolled Border Frame

Here's How:

1. **Quilling Instructions**

   For **Vine**:
   - Roll two 8" moss green paper strips into "S" scrolls. Using the open scroll technique, make the scrolls larger.

   - Roll two 4" moss green paper strips into "C" scrolls. Using the open scroll technique, make the scrolls larger.

   - Roll four 4" moss green paper strips into tight circles and four 2" moss green paper strips into tight circles. Refer to Tight Circle on pages 25–26.

   For **Heart**:
   - Roll two 6" pink paper strips into heart scrolls.

   For **Flower Buds**:
   - Roll four 6" ivory paper strips into half circles. Refer to Half Circle on page 25. Curve the points to make the shape of a flower bud.

   For **Leaves**:
   - Roll four 6" moss green paper strips into curved marquises. Refer to Marquise on page 25.

2. Make certain that you have all of the necessary quilled pieces.

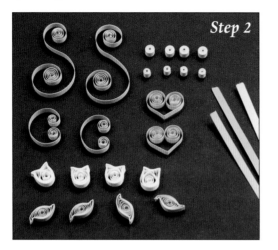

3. Arrange the scrolls and quilled shapes on the black mat as shown in 3a. Using the tweezers, pick up each piece and glue onto the mat.

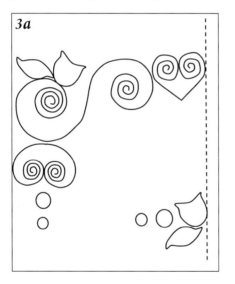

4. Mount the photograph to the mat and insert in the shadowbox.

Scroll Design Variations

Assemble, arrange, and position the scrolled pieces into any desired design. This is where you can use your imagination to play with the different scroll designs. When you finally have a design that fits the layout, use the tweezers to pick up each piece and glue into place on the mat.

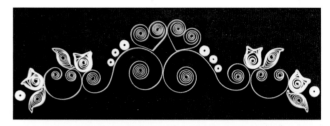

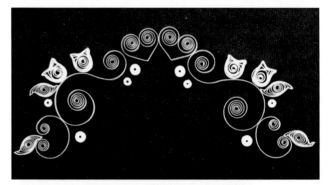

How do I use the "end-to-end" technique for different colored papers?

The end-to-end technique is taking two different colored paper strips, overlapping their ends, and gluing them together. It's very popular when making miniatures and colorful quilled pieces. With this technique, your imagination will run wild with possibilities.

4
Technique

What you need to get started:

- General Quilling Tools on pages 10–11

- ⅛"-wide quilling papers:
    black
    green
    light blue
    red
    white
    yellow

- Adhesive tabs

- Cardstock:
    dark blue
    light blue

- Paper trimmer with cutting blade

- Pencil and eraser

- Photograph

END-TO-END TECHNIQUE

1. Use two different colored paper strips. Place a dab of glue at the end of one paper strip.

2. Overlap the ends of the paper strips and press down to glue them together. *Note: Try to keep the paper strips straight by using a ruler or your quilling board as a guide.*

3. Roll the paper strip and make the desired quilled shape.

Technique Variation

A variation of the end-to-end technique is gluing the paper strips "side-to-side" as shown. With graduated-colored papers, the technique creates a great texture and shading.

Baby Boy Scrapbook Page

Here's How:

Finished size: 8" square

1. Cut an 8" square from dark blue cardstock for the scrapbook page.

2. Cut a 4" square from the light blue cardstock. Crop the photograph to 3¾" square and mount onto the light blue cardstock with adhesive tabs.

Step 2

3. Adhere the mounted photograph 1" down from the top of the scrapbook page.

4. **Quilling Instructions**

   For **Car**:
   - Roll a 12" green paper strip into a rectangle as shown in 4a. Refer to Rectangle on page 25.

   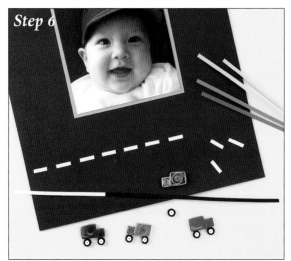

   4a

   - Roll a 6" green paper strip into a square. Refer to Square on page 25. Align at bottom and glue both pieces together as shown in 4a.

   For **Wheels**:
   - Glue a 6" black and a 3" white paper strip end-to-end. Make two sets. Starting from the white end, roll into tight circles. Refer to Tight Circle on pages 25–26. Glue the wheels to the bottom of the car as shown in 4a.

5. Repeat Step 4 three times to make a light blue car, a red car, and a yellow car.

6. To make the road lines, draw a pencil line 2" from the bottom of the scrapbook page. Cut ten ½"-long white paper strips and glue along the pencil line. If necessary, gently erase the pencil line between the white paper strips.

Step 6

7. Using the tweezers, pick up each car and glue onto the scrapbook page.

Car Variation

To make the adorable free-standing automobiles, use the same lengths listed in the project, but use ¼"- or ⅜"-wide strips. Adhere four wheels to the sides to have it stand upright.

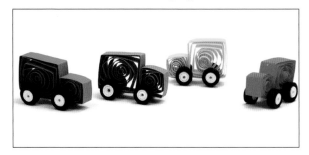

5
Technique

What you need
to get started:

- General Quilling Tools on pages 10–11
- ⅛"-diameter hole punch
- Burgundy cardstock
- Corkboard
- Pink embroidery floss
- Quilling papers:
  ⅛"-wide forest green
  ⅜"-wide pink

How do I make a folded rose?

The folded rose is a technique that uses 90-degree folds in the paper to form beautiful blooming roses. Typically, a wider paper strip is used to make this rose. It may take a few tries to see the petals take shape from the folded paper strips. This is one of those techniques where you might feel like you have all thumbs; but your patience and practice will be rewarded with incredible delicate roses that will amaze everyone.

FOLDED ROSE TECHNIQUE

1. Measure and tear an 8" strip from ⅜"-wide paper. Make a crease (fold) as a "place marker" about 1" from the paper's end. Using the slotted tool, roll the paper strip up to the crease, forming the center of the rose. *Note: The end of the paper strip should be pointing to the right and the rolled paper is facing you.*

Step 1

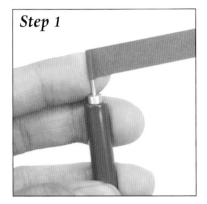

2. Fold the paper strip at a 90-degree right-angle so that the paper's end is pointed down, then as you rotate the tool around the fold, move the paper strip so that it is pointing to the right again.

Step 2a

Step 2b

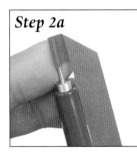

3. Repeat this same technique of first folding the end down 90 degrees, rotating the tool and paper strip around the tool to make a petal. *Note: Do not worry about the placement of the petals at this point because when the folds are completed, we will let the rose "bloom."*

Step 3a

Step 3b

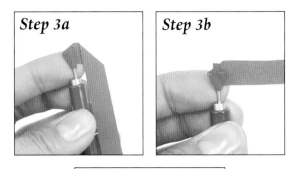

Step 3c

4. As you work away from the center, space out the folds farther apart. Continue to create the petals until you have reached the end of the paper strip.

Step 4

5. To finish the rose, fold over the paper strip one last time. Place the rose down on a flat surface and then let it "bloom" open. *Note: You can also use your fingers to unwind and open up the petals.* Glue the end of the paper strip to the rose.

Step 5a

Step 5b

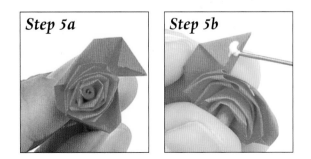

6. To help the petals and the center of the flower to stay in place, push the rose's rolled center down through the center of the rose so that it sticks out from the bottom. Spread glue around the bottom of the rose and let it dry.

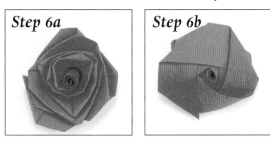

Step 6a

Step 6b

Step 6c

Folded Rose Variations

Try making folded roses with ¼"-wide paper.

Mini Rose Gift Tag

Here's How:

Finished size: 1" x 2"

1. Cut a 1" x 2" oval tag from burgundy cardstock.

2. Using a hole punch, make a hole for hanger in tag. Place the tag on a corkboard. Using the needle tool, pierce small holes along the edge.

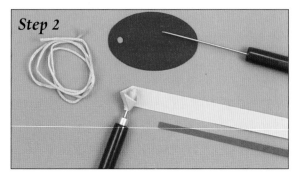

Step 2

3. **Quilling Instructions**

   For **Rose**:
   • Measure and tear an 8" pink strip from ⅜"-wide paper. Make into a folded rose as shown in 3a.

   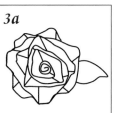

   3a

   For **Leaf**:
   • Roll a 6" forest green paper strip into a curved marquise. Refer to Marquise on page 25.

4. Glue the rose and leaf to the tag. Thread pink embroidery floss through the tag hole.

How do I make a curled petal rose?

Curled petal roses are made by layering small paper petals. There are two techniques to show the different looks between two types of petal shapes—rectangles and hearts. Heart and flower punches will be used in this project. Curled petal roses take a little more time to make, but the intricate details are stunning.

6
Technique

What you need to get started:

- General Quilling Tools on pages 10–11

- Paper punches:
  5-petal flower
  heart

- Papier-mâché boxes:
  round
  square

- Quilling papers:
  ⅛"-wide shades of green
  ⅛"-wide shades of pink
  ⅜"-wide pink

- Text-weight pink paper for punching

RECTANGLE CURLED PETAL ROSE TECHNIQUE

1. Start with a full length ⅜"-wide paper strip. Cut paper strips into nine rectangles about ½" in length. At one end of each piece, cut a slit into the paper to the center.

Step 1

2. Fold and overlap the two flaps. Then place a dab of glue between the two flaps and press them together. *Note: This makes the pieces "stand up," forming an upright petal.*

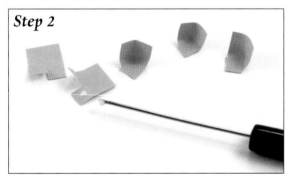

Step 2

3. Using the slotted tool, roll back, or curl the corners back.

Step 3

4. Punch a flower for the base of the rose. Using the tweezers, glue five rectangle petals onto the base to form the outer ring of petals.

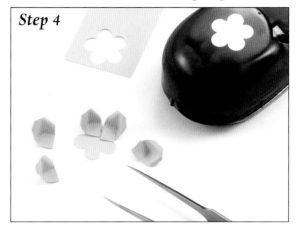

Step 4

5. Glue and place the four remaining petals on the inside of the rose.

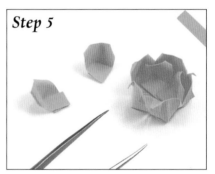

Step 5

6. To make the rose's center, use ⅛"-wide paper to roll a 4" paper strip into a loose circle. Refer to Loose Circle on page 25. Glue circle to the rose center.

Step 6

HEART CURLED PETAL ROSE TECHNIQUE

1. Using the heart punch, punch 12 hearts from a sheet of paper. Using the slotted tool, roll back, or curl, the two top curves of the heart. Bend the point of the heart punch-out to help the petals to "stand up." Repeat for each heart.

Step 1

2. Using the flower punch, punch out the base of the rose. Glue five heart petals to the flower base to form the outer ring of petals by using tweezers to hold the petal and to dip them in the puddle of glue. Glue four petals to form the middle ring of petals. Glue three more petals inside for the inner ring of petals.

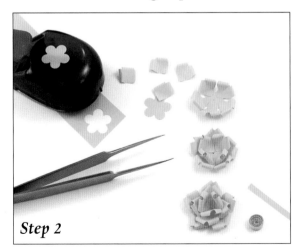

Step 2

3. To make the rose's center, use ⅛"-wide paper to roll a 4" paper strip into a loose circle. Refer to Loose Circle on page 25.

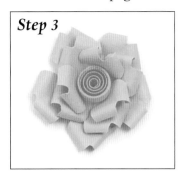

Step 3

Rose Variation

Try creating a curled petal rose made from punched heart petals and a small folded rose center. Refer to Folded Rose Technique on pages 39–40.

Curled Petal Variations

Simple punched out shapes, combined with quilled centers, can create unique and incredible flowers and roses. Use the slotted tool and tweezers to shape and curl each petal to make them look more realistic.

Keepsake Rose Boxes

Here's How:

1. **Quilling Instructions for Round Keepsake Box**

For **Rose**:
- Make a pink rectangle curled petal rose, using the petal size shown in 1a. Use a flower punch for base as shown in 1b.

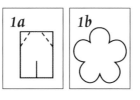

For **Leaves**:
- Roll six 4" green paper strips into marquises. Refer to Marquise on page 25.

2. Glue the rose to the center of the round box. Glue three leaves to each side of the rose as shown in 2a.

3. **Quilling Instructions Square Keepsake Box**

For **Rose**:
- Make a pink heart curled petal rose with hearts punched from pink sheets of paper as shown in 3a. Use a flower punch for the base of the rose as shown in 3b.

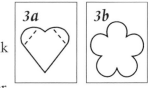

For **Leaves**:
- Roll two 8" green paper strips into curved marquises.

For **Scrolls**:
- Roll two 4" green paper strips into loose scrolls. Refer to Loose Scroll on page 32. Using the open scroll technique, make the scrolls larger. Refer to Open Scroll on page 33.

4. Glue the rose near a corner on the square box. Glue the two scrolls and leaves to the rose as shown in 4a.

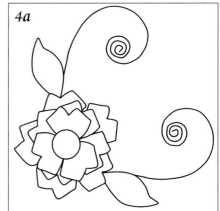

Note: Roses can be made with ¼"-wide paper or smaller heart-shaped punches, but it is easier to learn how to make them with wider paper or a larger size punch.

How do I make fringed flowers?

Fringing is one of the most popular and fascinating quilling techniques. There are so many variations to this technique than simply rolling it up. The technique is popular in creating flowers, and it's perfect for making animal fur, hat tassels, and more. Fringing can be done by hand, but a fringer is a worthwhile investment if you love these gorgeous flowers.

7
Technique

What you need to get started:

- General Quilling Tools on pages 10–11

- Adhesive tabs

- Cardstock:
    dark green
    light blue

- Fringer (optional)

- Light blue satin ribbon

- Quilling papers:
    ⅛"-wide light blue
    ⅛"-wide mint green
    ⅜"-wide bright green
        graduated

- Paper clamp (optional)

- Paper trimmer with cutting and scoring blades

FRINGING TECHNIQUE

1. Fringe an 8" paper strip from ⅜"-wide paper, using one of the following methods:

Method A:

• Fold the strip in half and use a paper clamp to secure ⅛" in from the paper's edge. *Note: Clamping the paper will prevent you from cutting all the way through the paper.* Cut slits along the exposed edge of the paper, starting from the fold. Unfold the paper strip and cut additional fringes at the fold if necessary.

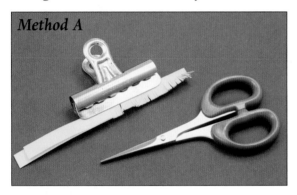

Method A

Method B:

• Insert the paper into the fringer. Use tweezers to help feed the paper under the springs that hold and advance the paper strip. Press the handle down to cut the paper. *Note: Fringers are designed to automatically advance the paper for the next cut.*

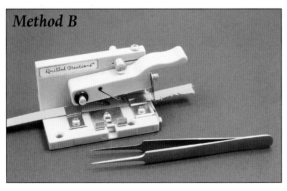

Method B

2. Rolling the uncut edge of the paper strip, roll a tight circle. Refer to Tight Circle on pages 25–26. Fluff the fringes outward by curling the fringes with the needle tool.

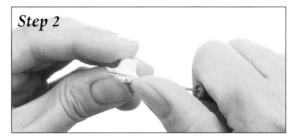

Step 2

Fringed Flower Variations

Basic Fringed Flower Method:

• Fringe a paper strip. Rolling the uncut edge of the paper strip, make a tight circle. Do not let it expand. Glue the end to the tight circle and fluff the fringes outward.

Flower with Angled Fringe Method:

• Fringe a paper strip. Trim the fringe at an angle on one end about 2" in length. Start rolling from the angled end. Do not let it expand. Glue the end to the tight circle and fluff the fringes outward. *Note: This technique makes the flower's center stand out better.*

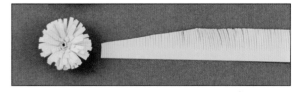

Multicolored Flower with Angled Fringe (Mums) Method:

- Fringe three different colored paper strips. Glue strips end-to-end. Refer to End-to-end Technique on page 36. Trim one fringed end at an angle. Start rolling from the angled end. Do not let it expand. Glue the end to the tight circle and fluff the fringes outward.

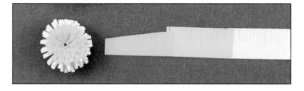

Flower with Angled Fringe & Center (Daisy) Method:

- Fringe a ⅜"-wide paper strip. Trim one fringed end at an angle about 2" in length. Glue a ⅛" width paper length "end-to-end" to the angled end. Start rolling from the ⅛" -wide paper. Do not let it expand. Glue the end to the tight circle and fluff the fringes outward.

Multicolored Flower with Angled Fringe & Center (Gerbera) Method:

- Fringe two paper strips of different shades, one ¼" wide and the other ⅜"-wide. Trim one fringed end with an angle. Glue a ⅛"-wide paper length to the angled end. Glue strips end-to-end with cut angle on end. Start rolling from the ⅛"-wide paper end. Do not let it expand. Glue the end to the tight circle and fluff the fringes outward.

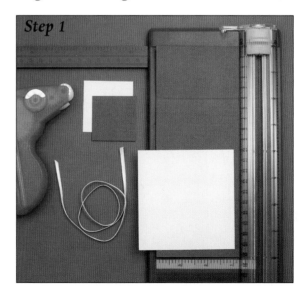

Gerbera Daisy Card

Here's How:

Finished size: 4" square

1. Cut a 4" x 8" card base and a 1¾" square from dark green cardstock. Cut a 2" square and a 3¾" square from the light blue cardstock. Cut a 20" length from the light blue satin ribbon.

Step 1

47

3. For the card base, score two lines 2" from each side and fold to form a trifold card. Center and mount the large light blue square to the inside of the card base with adhesive tabs. Mount the dark green square on the small light blue square.

4. Wrap the ribbon horizontally around the middle of the card. Use adhesive tab to secure the ribbon to one of the front side panels.

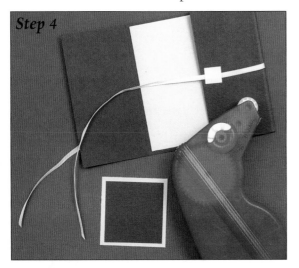

5. **Quilling Instructions**
   For **Gerbera Daisy**:
   - Fringe a 12" graduated bright green paper strip from ⅜"-wide paper. Trim the fringe at an angle on the green end. Glue ⅛"-wide 8" light blue paper strip end-to-end. Refer to End-to-end Technique on page 36. Start rolling from the light blue paper end and roll a tight circle. Refer to Tight Circle on pages 25–26. Fluff the fringes outward.

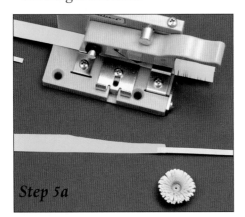

Step 5a

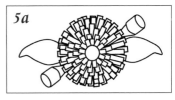

5a

- For leaves, roll two mint green 8" paper strips into curved marquises as shown in 5a. Refer to Marquise on page 25.

- For rolled buds, roll two 2" light blue paper strips into cone rolls. Refer to Cone Roll on page 26.

- Glue the gerbera daisy pieces onto the mounted green square.

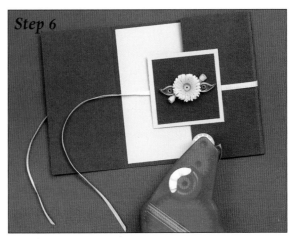

Step 5b

6. Mount the square with the quilled piece over the ribbon with adhesive tabs. Try to place the piece so that when the card is closed, the gerbera daisy is in the center of the card.

Step 6

7. Tie the ribbon into a bow to close the card.

Fringed Flowers with Added Embellishments

Chalk can be applied before or after fringing. If the paper is chalked before fringing, then add the chalk to the entire length and fringe the edge that is chalked. This will give the ends of your fringed flower a touch of color. If you add chalk after a flower is fringed, then add it to the top layer of petals near the center. This will give the fringed flower more depth.

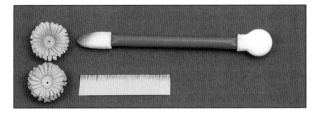

Like chalk, the ink adds highlights to the flower's edges. Draw the ink line along the edge of the fringe, then fringe the entire length of the paper strip.

Trim the length of the paper strip with decorative scissors, then fringe the entire length. The uneven edges will give a natural look to the flowers.

Try different printed papers to see what unique and unusual designs will result after fringing.

Roll graduated papers from either the dark or light colored end to see the different effects.

Try mixing and matching these added embellishments on the same flower. The possibilities are endless.

Below are close-up photographs of the fringed quilled pieces. For the lion's fur, see Noah's Ark on pages 86–89. For the lotus center, see Lotus Flower on page 101.

8 Technique

What you need to get started:

- General Quilling Tools on pages 10–11

- ⅛"-wide quilling papers:
    blue
    red
    white

- Chalk palettes:
    blue
    red

- Corkboard

- Foam-tipped chalk applicator

- Grid or graph paper (this project uses 5 squares per inch)

- Paper trimmer with cutting blade

- Pencil

- Printed verse or photograph

- Small wooden frame

- Straight pins (at least 5)

- Waxed paper or clear plastic bag

How do I use the husking technique?

The husking technique is simply taking quilling paper and wrapping it around pins. The diamond is a simple looping pattern. Once you see how simple the technique repeats, you can make just about any geometric shape. A fine-tipped glue bottle works great with this technique because you are constantly placing tiny drops of glue on the paper after each loop.

I can do *everything* through **HIM** who gives me **strength**.

Philippians 4:13

HUSKING TECHNIQUE

1. Using a pencil, trace a copy of the diamond pattern as shown in 1a. Place graph paper onto a corkboard protected by waxed paper or clear plastic bag to keep the glue from sticking to the pattern. *Note: This pattern will also be used for the project.*

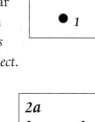

2. Make a small fold at one end of strip to aid in placement of the glue and the pin. Form a loop by placing a dab of glue between the fold as shown in 2a. Place a pin in the loop of the paper strip. Pin it down in Point #1 of the diamond pattern as shown in 1a.

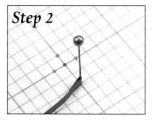

3. Place a pin in Point #2. Wrap the paper around that pin. Extend the paper down and around Pin #1. Glue the paper strip below Pin #1 to hold it in place. Repeat this around Pin #3 as shown in 3a.

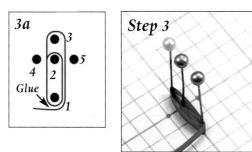

4. Place a pin in Point #4. Wrap the paper around Pin #4. Extend the paper down and around Pin #1. Glue between the paper strip below Pin #1 to hold it in place. Repeat around Pin #5 as shown in 4a.

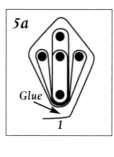

5. Wrap a collar around the outer pins. To help keep the shape of the husking pattern, place glue between the strips at each pin. Glue the strip below Pin #1 as shown in 5a. Trim off the excess paper.

TIP: When husking, place one pin at a time into the husking pattern. Glue below Pin #1 after each wrap to hold the loops together.

TIP: To prevent the tip of your glue bottle from clogging, place the bottle upside-down with the tip in a damp sponge.

Husking Pattern Variations

Create patterns with or without a grid. You can also wrap the collar around the pins without gluing it to the loops. This will make it easier to pinch the piece into different shapes.

Pattern Variations

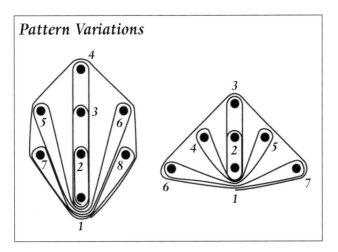

Patriotic Stars Frame

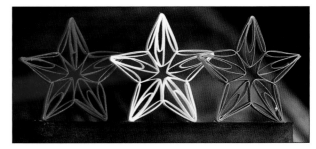

Here's How:

1. Apply blue and red chalk around edges of verse. Insert verse into the frame.

2. **Quilling Instructions**

   For **Star**:

   • Using a pencil, trace a diamond pattern on page 51 onto graph paper. Use five 8" red paper strips to husk the diamond pieces.

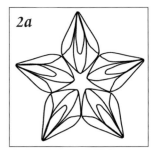

2a

   • Glue the five shorter points together to form the star as shown in 2a. Repeat to make a blue star and a white star.

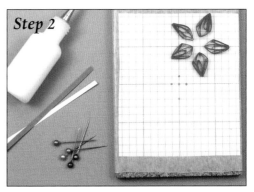

Step 2

3. Glue the three stars onto the wooden frame.

How do I use the alternate-side looping technique?

Alternate-side looping and wheatears looping is similar to husking, but the loops are made in your hands instead of with pins. The beauty of this method is the flexibility to make spectacular wing-like shapes and petals.

9
Technique

What you need to get started:

- General Quilling Tools on pages 10–11

- ⅛"-wide quilling papers:
  blue
  green
  light blue
  pumpkin or light brown

- 3"-diameter glass paperweight

- Black cardstock

Butterfly Paperweight

Here's How:

1. Cut the black cardstock to fit the bottom of the paperweight.

2. **Quilling Instructions**

   For **Butterfly**:

   • For wings, use the technique for alternate-side looping with three paper strips and make a large wing with four loops from blue, light blue and green papers as shown

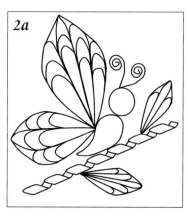

2a

   in 2a. Pinch a point on the wing. Make a smaller wing with three loops and pinch a point on the wing.

   • For body, roll an 8" light blue paper strip into a curved teardrop as shown in 2a. Refer to Teardrop on page 25.

   • For butterfly's head, roll a 4" light blue paper strip into a loose circle as shown in 2a. Refer to Loose Circle on page 25.

   • For antenna, roll a 2" light blue paper strip into "V" scroll where both scrolls are in the same direction as shown in 2a. Refer to "V" Scroll on page 32.

   For **Leaf**:

   • Using the alternate-side looping with single paper strip technique, make two small leaves from green paper.

   For **Twig**:

   • Roll a 4" pumpkin or light brown paper strip paper into a spiral. Trim to a 2" length as shown in 2a. Refer to Spiral on page 32.

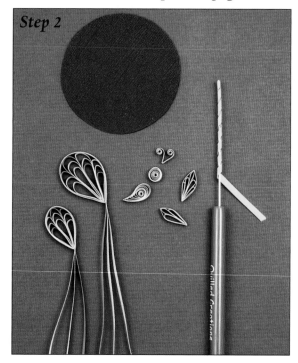

Step 2

3. Glue the wings and head to the body. Glue the antenna to the head.

4. Using tweezers, pick up and glue the butterfly, leaves, and twig onto the black cardstock.

5. Mount glass paperweight over the quilled pieces.

How do I braid and weave with quilling paper?

In this next technique, we'll apply two traditional techniques, braiding and weaving, with quilling paper. Braided or weaved paper is typically placed as a background or border on cards and frames. For this project, you'll make an adorable basket that can be filled with candy, flowers, or little treasures.

What you need to get started:

- General Quilling Tools on pages 10–11

- ⅛"-wide quilling papers:
    leaf green
    pink
    pumpkin

- Adhesive tabs

- Corkboard

- Grid or graph paper
    (5 squares per inch)

- Straight pins (at least 10)

- Waxed paper or
    transparent plastic bag

57

BRAIDING TECHNIQUE

1. Place a sheet of graph paper on a corkboard. Cover with waxed paper or clear plastic to protect it from glue. Secure three paper strips together as shown below. *Note: The graph paper will help align the paper strips after each fold.*

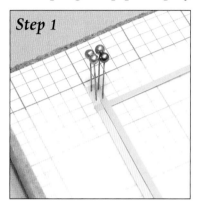

2. Fold over the pink paper strip on the left side 90 degrees.

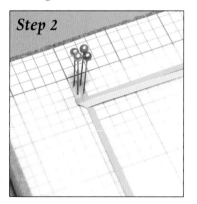

3. Place the moss green strip at the top and fold it over 90 degrees.

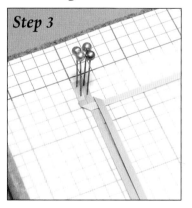

4. Continue alternating this pattern, forming the braid.

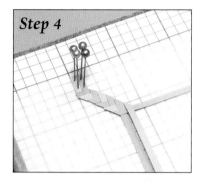

WEAVING TECHNIQUE

1. Place a sheet of graph paper on a corkboard. Cover with waxed paper or clear plastic to protect it from glue. Using the lines on the graph paper, align the paper strips vertically on the board. Secure each paper strip with two pins to prevent it from shifting.

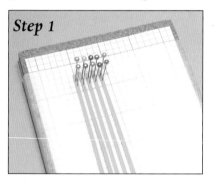

2. Using the lines on the graph paper to help align the paper strips vertically and horizontally, weave the horizontal strips over and under the vertical paper strips, adding glue where the strips intersect. Continue weaving until the desired size. Remove the pins. Trim to the desired shape and size.

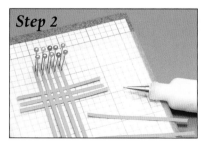

Miniature Woven Basket

Here's How:

1. Place the graph paper on a corkboard. Cover the board with waxed paper or a plastic bag to protect it from glue.

2. Pin five 8" pumpkin paper strips vertically on a grid. Weave approximately twenty 2" pumpkin paper strips horizontally, adding glue where the papers intersect. Glue the horizontal paper strips off-centered as shown below. Weave a 1" x 4" piece.

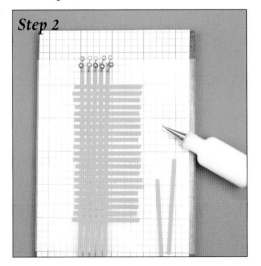

3. Trim the ends of the paper strips as shown, leaving 1" of the horizontal strips unwoven.

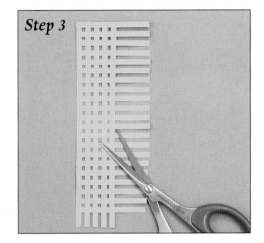

4. Fold over and crease the unwoven strips.

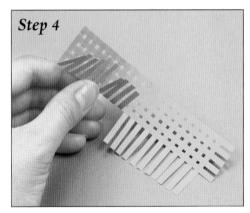

5. Bring the shorter sides of the weave together. Align and glue.

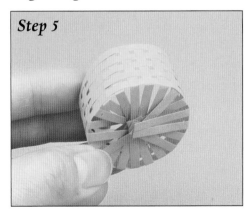

6. Glue the unwoven folded paper strips together.

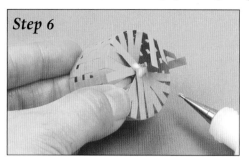

Step 6

7. To make the handle of the basket, braid three 8" pumpkin paper strips. Trim into a 3" length and glue to the inside of the basket.

Step 7

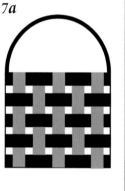

7a

8. **Quilling Instructions**

   For **Flower**:
   - Roll two 3" pink paper strips into curved teardrops as shown in 8a. Refer to Teardrop on page 25.

   For **Leaves**:
   - Roll two 3" leaf green paper strips into curved marquises as shown in 8a. Refer to Marquise on page 25.

8a

9. Glue the flower and the leaves to the basket.

Step 9

Basket Variations

Create other basket designs by mixing and matching different colored paper strips together.

Add unique embellishments to each basket.

The picnic blanket featured on the above card was created by weaving red and white paper strips. The basket was created by using the braiding technique.

How do I boondoggle with quilling paper?

Boondoggle is a technique that is usually done with fibers or plastic strands. When I first tried the classic knot with quilling paper, I wasn't quite sure what to do with the results. But with some creativity, I found that you can create some exciting pieces.

BOONDOGGLING TECHNIQUE

The easiest method of explaining boondoggling is by assigning quadrants and numbers to the paper strips.

1. Take two paper strips and glue to form a cross. *Note: The photographs show different quadrants and numbered paper strips. This will show you where each paper strip will be placed.*

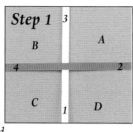

2. Fold Strip #1 into Quadrant A. Fold Strip #2 into Quadrant B. Fold Strip #3 into Quadrant C.

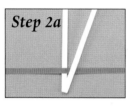 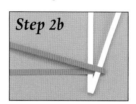

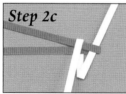

3. Fold Strip #4 over and under the white paper strips to Quadrant D.

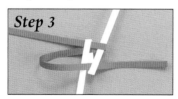

4. Gently pull all of the paper strips tight to flatten and form a classic knot. Repeat Steps 2–4 to desired length.

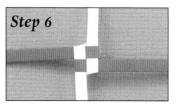

Candy Cane Ornament

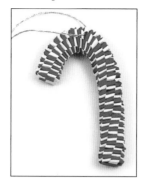

Here's How:

1. **Quilling Instructions**

   For **Candy Cane**:
   - Boondoggle a full length of a red and a white paper strip. *Note: When you need more paper, glue the new paper strips end-to-end as you go. Refer to End-to-end Technique on page 36.* Continue boondoggling until candy cane is the desired size as shown in 1a. Fold over and glue paper ends. Curve one end of boondoggle to form top.

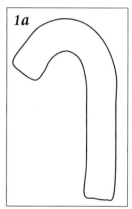

2. Attach a thread to the candy cane for hanger.

Boondoggling Variations

Shown here are some ideas on how you can use the boondoggling technique.

What is the combing, or onion holder, technique?

This technique uses a wide-toothed comb or an onion holder to weave the paper into different shapes. In Europe, this technique is known as spreuer. The results are elongated loops that make wonderful, cascading shapes. The spacing between the prongs will either give you a small piece or a larger shape. Try it with graduated-color papers to see the striking effect.

12
Technique

What you need to get started:

- General Quilling Tools on pages 10–11

- ⅛"-wide quilling papers:
  deep yellow
  light blue
  lilac
  mint green
  yellow

- Black cardstock

- Onion holder

- Paper trimmer with cutting and scoring blades

ONE-SIDE COMBING TECHNIQUE

1. Wrap the paper's end around the top two prongs of the onion holder and place a dab of glue on the paper strip at the top.

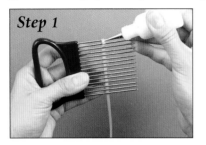
Step 1

2. Count down eight prongs and loop the paper strip around it. Bring it back to the top and glue into place. *Note: This is called the "center" loop.*

Step 2

3. Loop the paper strip around the seventh prong. Place a dab of glue at the top and glue into place.

Step 3

4. Repeat this technique on one side, reducing each successive loop by one prong.

Step 4

ALTERNATING-SIDES COMBING TECHNIQUE

1. Wrap the paper's end around the top two prongs of the onion holder and place a dab of glue on the paper strip at the top. Count down eight prongs and loop the paper strip around it. Bring it back to the top and glue into place. *Note: This is called the "center" loop.*

Step 1

2. Loop the paper strip around the seventh prong on the right side of the "center" loop and glue it at the top.

Step 2

3. Feed and loop the paper around the seventh prong again, but on the left side of the "center" loop and glue into place.

Step 3

4. Repeat this technique of alternating sides and gluing after each loop until desired size is achieved.

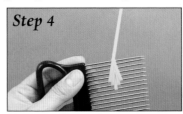
Step 4

Hummingbird & Buttercup

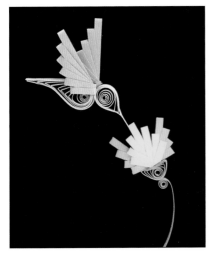

Here's How:

Finished size: 4" x 5½"

1. Cut a 5½" x 8" card base from black cardstock. Score and fold in half to the finished size.

2. **Quilling Instructions**

   For **Hummingbird**:

   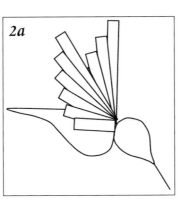

   - For wings, make a six-looped, or "feathered" one-sided wing from a full-length lilac paper strip, using the one-sided combing technique. Repeat for second wing.

     Note: The size of the wing will depend on the spacing of the prongs.

   - For the head, roll a 6" light blue paper strip into a teardrop. Refer to Teardrop on page 25.

   - For the beak, fold a 1" light blue paper strip in half.

   - For the body, roll a 16" light blue paper strip into a narrow teardrop with a very flat point for the hummingbird's tail as shown in 2a.

For **Buttercup**:

- For the side petals, make two four-looped petals from full-length deep yellow paper strips, using one-sided combing technique. Make the center petal from a full-length yellow paper strip as shown in 2b, using alternating-sides combing technique.

- For the calyx, roll a 6" mint green paper strip into a half circle. Refer to Half Circle on page 25.

- For the stem, roll half of a 3" mint green strip into a loose scroll. Refer to Loose Scroll on page 32.

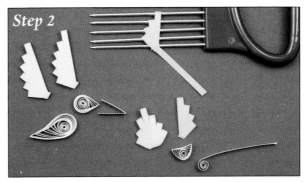

3. To assemble the hummingbird, first glue the beak onto the head at the point of the teardrop. Glue the head and body together. Glue one wing (rear), just above the head and body. Layer and glue the front wing on top of the body.

4. To assemble the buttercup, glue the three petals together with the center petal layered on top of the side petals. Glue the calyx and stem to the petals.

5. Center and glue the quilled pieces onto the card.

13
Technique

What you need to get started:

- General Quilling Tools on pages 10–11

- ⅛"-wide quilling papers:
  brown
  forest green
  ivory
  leaf green
  orange
  purple
  red
  yellow

- Brown fine-tipped felt pen

- Waxed paper or plastic bag

- Marble to help shape pieces

How do I make miniatures from tight circles?

Miniatures are achieved by first making tight circles or flat disks and transforming them into three-dimensional objects. Once you are comfortable with this technique, you'll be delighted with the limitless combinations that can be created, ranging from flowerpots to miniature figurines.

MAKING MINIATURES

Before beginning to make miniatures please familiarize yourself with the following information:

Paper Surface Direction

All precision cut quilling papers have a smooth side where the cut edges are rounded or slightly turned down. When flipped over, the cut edges are more visible. When gluing multiple strips of the same color end-to-end, it's important to glue the smooth side facing all in the same direction. Refer to the End-to-end Technique on page 36. After rolling a large tight circle, it will look like one continuous piece. See photograph below. *Note: When you take paper strips out of its packaging, keep track of the smooth side before gluing them together.*

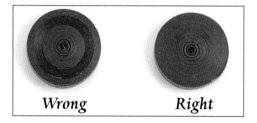

Wrong   *Right*

Tear Both Ends

When gluing paper strips end-to-end, tear the ends of both strips. The torn or feathered ends make the transition between strips less visible.

Fine-tipped Tweezers

Take advantage of using tweezers to pinch, shape, pick up, and assemble the miniature.

Paper Thickness

All papers are made differently with slight different thicknesses. Two different colored papers may roll to a different size roll. For large tight circles, the final diameter measurement is given to help you achieve the right sized piece.

Dome

1. Using the slotted tool, roll large tight circles. Refer to Tight Circle on pages 25–26. Hold your fingers flat against the roll as you rotate the tool. Roll using light, but even tension.

Step 1

2. After rolling the tight circle, glue the end to the tight circle. To even out the paper edges, use the handle of the tool like a rolling pin and roll the quilled tight circle like piecrust. *Note: This will make it easier to shape your pieces.*

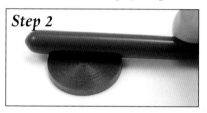

Step 2

3. To shape a large tight circle into a dome, use your fingers to push out the center as you rotate the piece in your other hand.

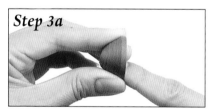

Step 3a

TIP: For small tight circles, shape the roll with the end of the quilling tool, a tip of the bottle, marbles, tweezers, and other objects as shown in 3b.

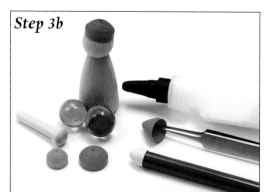

Step 3b

4. To keep the shape of the dome, spread a generous layer of glue on the inside or outside. Let it dry.

Step 4

Miniature Fruit Bowl

Here's How:

1. **Quilling Instructions**

   For **Peeled Banana**:
   - Roll two 4" ivory paper strips into cone rolls as shown in 1a. Refer to Cone Roll on page 26. Glue together.

   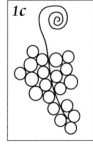
   1a

   - Cut five 1" yellow paper strips. Trim to make the ends pointed as shown in 1a. Using the brown pen, color the ends and make spots on the banana peels. Glue the peels to the banana.

   For **Apple**:
   - Glue red paper strips end-to-end to create two 36" paper strips. Refer

   1b

to End-to-end Technique on page 36. Roll into tight circles as shown in 1b. Refer to Tight Circle on pages 25–26. Shape the top and bottom halves of the apple with a marble. Spread glue on the inside surface and let it dry. Glue the two halves together.

- Roll a 1" brown paper strip into a cone shape for stem. Cut a small leaf from leaf green paper. Glue stem and leaf to apple.

For **Orange**:
- Using orange paper strips, follow the Apple instructions. Cut a small green piece for the top of the orange and glue to the top. Using a brown felt-tipped pen, make a brown spot for the stem.

For **Grapes**:
- For the stem, roll a 2" brown paper strip into a loose scroll as shown in 1c. Refer to Loose Scroll on page 32.

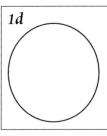
1c

- For the grapes, tear approximately 30 purple paper strips about 2"–3" in length. Roll into tight circles. On waxed paper, randomly glue the grapes to the stem as shown in 1c. Glue a second layer of grapes on top at different angles.

For **Bowl**:
- Glue full-length about 160", or ten 16" forest green paper strips end-to-end. Roll a 1" diameter tight circle as shown in 1d. Even out the edges by rolling the handle of the tool over the top like rolling out piecrust. Using your finger, shape the bowl as shown in 1e. Spread glue on the inside surface and let it dry.

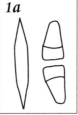
1d

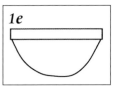
1e

2. Arrange fruit in and around bowl as desired.

How do I use the crimping technique?

Crimping gives dramatic texture, or the "zigzag" look, to your paper strip. When rolling a long, crimped paper strip, the roll dynamically changes as you twist it tighter. This technique definitely brings quilling with paper to another level of excitement.

What you need to get started:

- General Quilling Tools on pages 10–11

- 6" high x 3½" diameter glass candleholder

- Clear tape

- Corkboard

- Crimpers:
    large
    small

- Moveable craft eye

- Paper trimmer with cutting blade

- Quilling papers:
    ⅛"-wide deep blue
    ⅛"-wide deep yellow
    ⅛"-wide light blue
    ⅛"-wide pale yellow
    ⅛"-wide peach
    ⅛"-wide yellow
    ⅜"-wide deep blue
    ⅜"-wide deep yellow

- Vellums:
    blue
    green
    white / speckled

- Votive candle

CRIMPING TECHNIQUE

1. Using the crimper, crimp the paper strip.

2. Using slotted tool, roll the paper strip with light pressure to prevent the crimps from flattening.

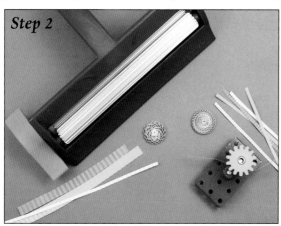

Step 2

Seaside Candleholder

Here's How:

1. Cut a 6" x 11" rectangle from the green vellum.

2. Cut a 4" x 11" rectangle from the white vellum. Tear one side along the 11" length.

3. Cut a 2" x 11" rectangle from the blue vellum. Tear one side along the 11" length.

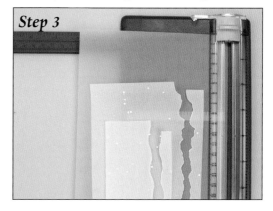

Step 3

4. **Quilling Instructions**

   For **Sun**:

   • Glue one each of ⅛"-wide 16" pale yellow, 16" yellow, and 16" deep yellow paper strips end-to-end. Refer to End-to-end Technique on page 36. Crimp

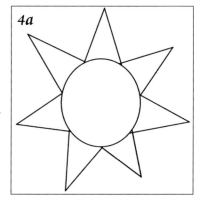

4a

the entire length with the small crimper. Using the slotted tool and light pressure, start rolling from the pale yellow end and roll it into a tight circle as shown in 4a. Refer to Tight Circle on pages 25–26.

   • For rays, crimp a ⅜"-wide 6" deep yellow paper strip with the large crimper. Cut strip into seven triangles. Glue to the sun.

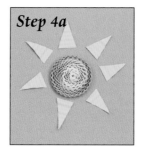

Step 4a

For **Fish:**

- For the body, use the small crimper to crimp one each of ⅛"-wide 16" deep yellow, 16" light blue, and 16" deep blue paper strips. Layer and glue the three paper strips together at one end. Using the slotted tool, roll the three paper strips at the same time into a loose circle. Refer to Loose Circle on page 25. Trim off any excess lengths and form into an off-centered circle. Refer to Off-centered Circle Technique on page 29. Pinch into a teardrop. Refer to Teardrop on page 25.

- For fish's lips, roll two 4" deep yellow paper strips into teardrops. Glue to the fish's body.

- For fins and tail fin, use the large crimper to crimp ⅜"-wide 4" deep blue paper strip. Cut into three fins and a tail fin as shown in 4b. Glue the fins and tail fin to the body.

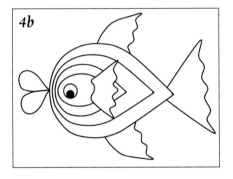

4b

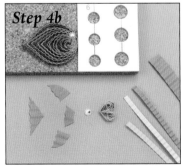

Step 4b

For **Seashell:**

- Using the small crimper, crimp two each of 16", 12" and 8" peach paper strips. Roll the 16" and 12" paper strips into teardrops as shown in 4c. Roll the 8" paper strips into triangles. Refer to Triangle on page 25.

4c

- Glue the pieces together to make the seashell.

5. Layer the three vellum papers together. Place clear tape at the ends of the vellum papers to hold them together. *Note: Taping the vellum is preferred so that the sheets will lay flat. The wetness of the glue will warp and buckle the vellum's edges.*

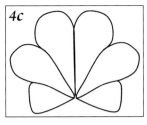

Step 5

6. Glue the sun, seashell, and fish to the center of the vellum.

Step 6

7. Wrap the entire piece around the candleholder and tape it in place. Place a votive candle inside the holder.

Section 3: *Beyond the Basics*

1
Project

What you need to get started:

- General Quilling Tools on pages 10–11

- ⅛"-wide crimson satin ribbon

- Adhesive tabs

- Cardstock:
    beige
    white

- Corkboard

- Hole punch

- Quilling papers:
    ⅛"-wide crimson
    ⅛"-wide forest green
    ⅛"-wide leaf green
    ⅛"-wide red
    ⅛"-wide white
    ⅛"-wide yellow
    ⅜"-wide leaf green

- Paper trimmer with cutting and scoring blades

- Photograph

- Silver embroidery thread

- Watercolor paints:
    gold
    iridescent green

- Waxed paper or plastic bag

How do I make quilled Christmas ornaments and tags?

These projects are just a small sample of what you can make for the holiday season. Quilled snowflakes make perfect photographed tokens to embellish your tree. Elegant tags will receive many "oohs and ahhs" from the grateful gift-receiver. The adorable little Christmas tree makes a festive table decor too.

Christmas Ornaments & Tags

Here's How:

CHRISTMAS TREE

1. **Quilling Instructions**

   For **Christmas Tree**:

   1a

   • For trunk, roll three 8" leaf green strips from ⅛"-wide paper into tight circles. Refer to Tight Circle on pages 25–26. Glue together to form a trunk as shown in 1a.

   • For branches, roll six each of 4", 6", 8", and 12" leaf green strips from ⅛"-wide paper into curved teardrops. Refer to Teardrop on page 25. Glue one of each of the four different-sized tear-drops together to make one set of branches as shown in 1a. Make six sets.

   • For treetop, roll an 8" leaf green strip from ⅛"-wide paper into a teardrop.

   For **Star**:

   • Roll a 6" yellow paper strip into a tight circle.

   For **Berries**:

   • Roll nine 2" red paper strips into tight circles.

2. Glue the six branches to the trunk. Glue the treetop and star to top of trunk. Randomly, glue berries to the branches as shown in 1a.

Step 2

SNOWFLAKE ORNAMENT

1. Crop a 1½" circle from a photograph.

2. **Quilling Instructions**

   Note: Use the circle template board to help make uniform shapes.

   For **Snowflake**:

   • For center, roll six 8" white paper strips into teardrops. For middle, roll six 8" white paper strips into off-centered circles as shown in 2a on page 76. Refer to Off-centered Circle Technique on page 29.

- For outer points, roll twelve 4" white paper strips into off-set "S" scrolls as shown in 2a. Refer to "S" Scroll on page 32.

- For snowflake point, roll six 4" white paper strips into teardrops as shown in 2a.

- Roll six 4" white paper strips into scrolled hearts as shown in 2b. Refer to Heart Scroll on page 32.

2a

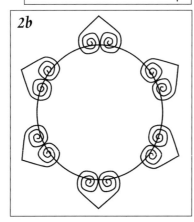

2b

3. To make the snowflake uniform and symmetrical, use paper marked with 60-degree angles. Place on a waxed-paper- or plastic-covered corkboard and use pins to hold the pieces in place.

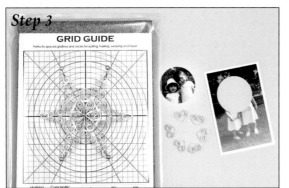

Step 3

GRID GUIDE

4. Glue center pieces first and work outward. Glue photograph to the center of the snowflake. Glue scrolled hearts onto snowflake and photograph as shown in photograph on page 75.

Step 4

5. Insert silver thread through top of snowflake, creating a loop for hanger.

HOLLY BERRY TAG

Finished size: 2" x 4"

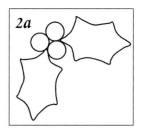

1. Cut a 2" x 4" rectangle from beige cardstock. Trim the corners and punch a hole centered at one end to create a tag.

2. **Quilling Instructions**
   For **Holly Leaves**:
   - Roll two 12" forest green paper strips into curved hexagons as shown in 2a. Refer to Hexagon on page 25.

   2a

   For **Berries**:
   - Roll three 6" crimson paper strips into tight circles for berries as shown in 2a.

For **Corner Berries**:
- Roll three 4" crimson paper strips into tight circles.

For **Border**:
- Roll a 16" forest green paper strip into a spiral. Refer to Spiral on page 32. Trim to fit around the tag.

3. Glue holly leaves and berries to one tag corner and the small corner berries in the remaining corners. Glue the spirals between the holly and berries.

4. Fold crimson ribbon in half. Insert through hole in end of the tag. Knot to secure.

POINSETTIA CARD

Finished size: 3" square

1. Cut a 3" x 6" card base from white cardstock. Score and fold in half to the finished size.

2. **Quilling Instructions**

   For **Poinsettia**:
   - Roll nine 8" red paper strips into marquises. Refer to Marquise on page 25. Glue three marquises together where two are glued at an angle and on top of the center petal as shown in 2a. Make three sets.
   - For center, cut 2" yellow paper strip in half lengthwise to make a $\frac{1}{16}$"-wide paper strip. Trim into three 1" strips and roll into loose scrolls as shown in 2a. Refer to Loose Scroll on page 32.
   - For leaves, roll two 12" leaf green strips from $\frac{1}{8}$"-wide paper into curved marquises as shown in 2a.
   - For scrolls, roll two 3" leaf green strips from $\frac{1}{8}$"-wide paper into loose scrolls as shown in 2a.

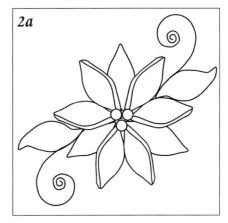

2a

3. Glue the petal sets to the card center. Glue the flower's center, leaves, and scrolls onto the card.

4. To make the flower sparkle, add gold and iridescent green watercolor paints to the edges.

Step 4

2 Project

What you need to get started:

- General Quilling Tools on pages 10–11

- 3mm diameter pearls (4)

- 8" x 10" shadowbox with a burgundy mat

- Foam-tipped chalk applicator

- Fringer

- Light pink text-weight paper

- Quilling papers:
  ⅛"-wide dusty rose
  ⅛"-wide ivory
  ⅛"-wide moss green
  ⅛"-wide orchid
  ⅛"-wide pale yellow
  ¼"-wide pale pink
  ¼"-wide raspberry
  ⅜"-wide dusty rose

- Pink or fuchsia chalk palette

How do I quill a framed wedding invitation?

For this wedding invitation, I tried to incorporate a variety of popular flowers that are in weddings. Before I make a quilled frame, I first like to ask the bride what flowers she will be holding in her bouquet and what colors are in her wedding. It gives a special personal touch to the bride and groom when they open this gift.

Wedding Invitation

Here's How:

1. Quilling Instructions

For **Calla Lilies**:

• Cut out four teardrop shapes from light pink paper as shown in 1a. Add a little chalk to the centers. Pinch and glue a moss green stem to bottom of each teardrop. Make two calla lilies with 3" stems and two with 2" stems.

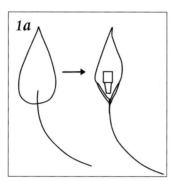

• For calla lilies' centers, use ⅛"-wide paper to roll four 1" pale yellow paper strips into cone rolls. Refer to Cone Roll on page 26. Glue to the centers of the calla lilies as shown in 1a.

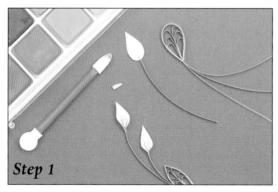

Step 1

For **Looped Leaf**:

• Use the alternate-sided looping technique to make two looped leaves as shown in 1b. Refer to Alternate-side Looping with Multiple Paper Strips on pages 54–55. Glue three full-length moss green paper strips and form two loops, wrapped with a collar. Pinch a point to form the leaf shape. Make four leaves.

For **Fringed Flowers**:

• Use ¼"-wide paper to fringe an 8" raspberry paper strip. Refer to Fringing Technique on pages 46–47. Cut into four 2" strips. Trim an angle on one end. Roll from the shorter end to form a tight circle. Fluff the fringes outward as shown in 1c. Make four raspberry flowers.

• Use ¼"-wide paper to fringe a 16" pale pink paper strip. Cut into four 4" strips. Trim an angle on one end. Roll from the shorter end to form a tight circle. Fluff the fringes outward as shown in 1d. Make four pale pink flowers.

For **Daisy**:

• Roll six 8" ivory paper strips into off-centered circles. Refer to Off-centered Circle Technique on page 29. Pinch into teardrops as shown in 1e. Refer to Teardrops on page 25.

• For the center, use 8" length strip of ¼"-wide pale pink paper to make a folded rose as shown in 1f. Refer to Folded Rose Technique on pages 39–40. Glue folded rose to daisy's center.

For **Rose**:

• Use ⅜"-wide dusty rose paper strips to make two rectangular curled petal roses as shown in 1g. Refer to Rectangle Curled Petal Rose Technique on page 42.

For **Small Flowers**:

• Roll twenty 2" orchid paper strips into marquises as shown in 1h. Refer to Marquise on page 25. Glue five marquises together. Make four flowers. Glue one pearl to the center of each flower as shown in 1h.

1h

For **Leaves**:

• Roll eight 6" moss green paper strips into curved marquises as shown in 1i.

1i

For **Scrolls**:

• Roll six 4" moss green paper strips into loose scrolls. Refer to Loose Scroll on page 32. Using the open scroll technique, make the scrolls larger as shown in 1j. Refer to Open Scroll Technique on page 33.

1j

Step 1

2. Arrange and glue the pieces onto the mat as shown in 2a.

2a

How do I quill floral letters?

Floral letters are designed with basic scrolls. Add a variety of simple flowers and quilled leaves between the scrolls. This project has the letters "LOVE" embellished with quilled flowers. The same technique can be used for the entire alphabet.

3 Project

What you need to get started:

- General Quilling Tools on pages 10–11

- 5"-square frame

- Adhesive tabs

- Burgundy cardstock

- Paper trimmer with cutting blade

- Pink toile patterned paper

- Quilling papers:
  ⅛"-wide ivory
  ⅛"-wide moss green
  ⅛"-wide three shades
   of pink
  ¼"-wide ivory
  ¼"-wide shades of pink

"LOVE" Frame

Here's How:

1. Cut a 5" square from the patterned paper.

2. Cut four 2¼" squares from the burgundy cardstock. Tear the edges of the cardstock squares so that the final size is approximately 2" square.

3. **Quilling Instructions**

   Notes: Use ⅛"-wide paper, except for the rose.
   For this project, you can use different colors for each of your flowers. All of the flowers in the "LOVE" are made using the same method. Therefore, the instructions below give only the paper lengths and quilled shape, not quantity or color.

   ### For **Rose**:
   - Use ¼"-wide paper to fold a 6" strip paper into a folded rose as shown in 3a. Refer to Folded Rose Technique on pages 39–40.

   ### For **Rosebud**:
   - Roll a 3" paper strip into a curved teardrop as shown in 3b. Refer to Teardrop on page 25.

   ### For **Leaf**:
   - Roll a 3" moss green paper strip into a marquise as shown in 3c. Refer to Marquise on page 25.

   ### For **Rolled Bud**:
   - Roll a 2" paper strip into a cone roll as shown in 3d. Refer to Cone Roll on page 26.

For Letters:

- For "L", roll two 3" moss green paper strips into "S" scrolls where the middle of the strip is straight as shown in 3e. Refer to "S" Scroll on page 32. Add a rose, a rosebud, three rolled buds, and three leaves.

- For "O", roll two 4" moss green paper strips into "C" scrolls. Refer to "C" Scroll on page 32. Unroll the scroll to form the desired size circle as shown in 3f. Add a rose, a flower bud, two rolled buds, and two leaves.

- For "V", roll two 3" moss green paper strips into "S" scrolls where the middle of the strip is straight as shown in 3g. Add a rose, a flower bud, three rolled buds, and three leaves.

- For "E", roll three 3" moss green paper strips into "S" scrolls where the middle of the strip is straight as shown in 3h. Add a rose, a flower bud, two rolled buds, and three leaves.

3h

6. Mount the squares to the patterned paper.

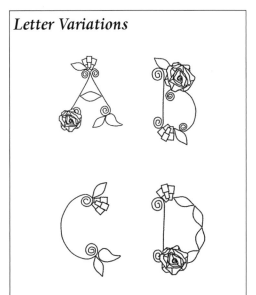

Step 5

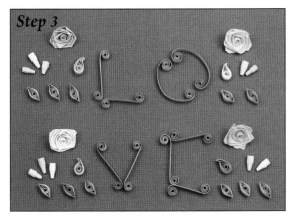

Step 3

For **Pegs**:

- Roll sixteen 8" paper strips into tight circles. Using the side of the tool, roll over the edges to flatten and even out the peg.

4. Glue the scrolled lettering, flowers, and leaves to the burgundy squares.

5. Glue the pegs to the back side of each square to raise the piece up and away from background.

Step 4

Quilled Floral Letter Variations

To make other alphabet letters, use quilled basic shapes, scrolls, and folded roses to arrange a floral letter pattern. Refer to Basic Shapes Technique on pages 25–26, Basic Scroll Techniques on page 32, and Folded Rose Technique on pages 39–40. Try different combinations to form the shape of the letter and accent with smaller flowers.

Letter Variations

4

Project

What you need to get started:

- General Quilling Tools on pages 10–11

- Adhesive tabs

- Black fine-tipped permanent marker

- Dark plum cardstock

- Foam-tipped chalk applicator

- Fuchsia or pink chalk palette

- Leaf stamp with olive inkpad

- Light green gingham patterned paper

- Paper trimmer with cutting blade

- Paper punches:
  5-petal flower
  heart

- Photographs:
  baby
  baby's feet

- Quilling papers:
  ⅛"-wide pink
  ¼"-wide pink

- Text-weight papers:
  lilac
  pink

How can I combine quilling with scrapbooking and stamping?

What little treasures are tiny newborn babies and the quilled baby's feet. The texture, flexibility, and look of stamping along with quilled flowers are beautiful. There are endless possibilities with scrapbooking and stamping. Let the photograph be your guide and use quilling pieces to highlight the subject.

Baby's Feet Page

Here's How:

Finished size: 8" square

1. Cut an 8" square from dark plum cardstock as the scrapbook page background.

2. On 4" x 6" lilac paper, use black marker and write the text around the photograph, "Each and every feature a miracle to see, you are the sweetest little girl that there could ever be." *Note: The text can be computer generated.*

3. Crop the baby photograph to fit between the text and mount it with adhesive tabs. Crop the feet photograph to about 2" square.

4. On a 2" lilac square, print the text "Oh, how sweet are little feet!"

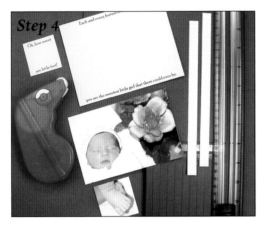
Step 4

4. Cut two 8" x ½" rectangles strips from gingham patterned paper.

5. Stamp two leaves on moss green paper. Trim around the stamped leaves.

Step 5

6. **Quilling Instructions**

   For **Baby's Feet**:
   • With ⅛"-wide paper, roll four 8" pink paper strips into curved teardrops as shown in 6a. Refer to Teardrop on page 25. For the toes, roll two 4", two 3", and six 2" paper strips into tight circles. Refer to Tight Circle on pages 25–26.

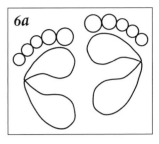
6a

   For **Rose**:
   • For petals, punch nine hearts from a pink sheet of paper. Chalk the rose petals with fuchsia chalk. Make the base of the rose using the curled petal rose technique as shown in 6b. Refer to Heart Curled Petal Rose Technique on page 43. Repeat for the second rose.

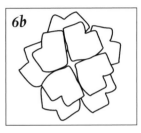
6b

   • For the center, use ¼"-wide paper and 8" length pink paper strip to make a folded rose as shown in 6c. Refer to Folded Rose Technique on pages 39–40. Repeat for second rose

6c

Step 6

7. Add a little more fuchsia chalk to top of the folded rose.

8. Mount quilled pieces onto the scrapbook page as shown in photograph on page 84.

5
Project

What you need to get started:

- General Quilling Tools on pages 10–11

- 5" x 7" wooden frame

- Adhesive tabs

- Black fine-tipped felt pen

- Cardstock:
    light blue
    brown

- Corkboard

- Moveable eyes (4 sets)

- Paper trimmer with cutting blade

- Quilling papers:
    ⅛"-wide black
    ⅛"-wide blue
    ⅛"-wide brown
    ⅛"-wide deep yellow
    ⅛"-wide leaf green
    ⅛"-wide light gray
    ⅛"-wide pumpkin
    ⅛"-wide white
    ¼"-wide brown
    ¼"-wide pumpkin

- Straight pins (at least 16)

- Waxed paper

How do I quill animals?

Don't rock the boat! This floating zoo will fascinate and delight any child. Like Noah, you'll enjoy "building" this ark all by yourself and filling it with adorable quilled creatures.

Noah's Ark Frame

Here's How:

1. Cut a 5" x 7" rectangle from the light blue card-stock for the background.

2. Cut a 1½" square from the brown cardstock. *Note: The lion will be glued to this piece and placed behind the open window in the ark.*

3. **Quilling Instructions**

   For **Ark**:

   Note: The ark is made from ¼"-wide quilling paper. Use a waxed-paper-covered corkboard with graph paper to help keep the pieces straight.

   - For the top portion, pin and secure five 3" brown paper strips horizontally. For the bottom portion, pin eight 5" brown paper strips horizontally as shown at right.

   Step 3a

   - For the top, weave and glue one at a time, two 2" brown paper strips vertically about 1½" apart. Refer to Weaving Technique on pages 58–59. For the bottom, weave and glue one at a time, four 3" brown paper strips vertically,

   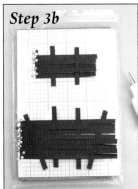

   Step 3b

   about 1½" apart at the top. Glue the vertical strips at the intersections with a fine-tipped glue bottle. *Note: The two vertical side strips on the ark's bottom portion are placed at an angle.*

- Trim the ends to form the pattern of the ark shown in 3a on page 88.

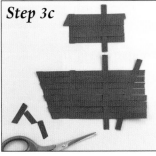

Step 3c

- To make the open window, cut four horizontal center strips down the middle. On one side, fold the four horizontal strips out. Glue a 1" paper strip vertically to hold them together. Repeat for the remaining side.

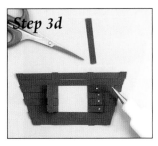

Step 3d

- Using a black felt-tipped pen, add the dots or "nail heads" to some of the intersections.

- For pegs, roll eight 8" brown strips from ⅛"-wide paper into tight circles. Refer to Tight Circle on pages 25–26. Glue onto the back of the ark bottom.

Step 3e

For **Elephant**:

- For body, glue light gray strips end-to-end to make a 32" strip. Refer to End-to-end Technique on page 36. Roll and place in the circle template board to form it into an off-centered circle. Refer to Off-centered Circle Technique on page 29.

- For head, roll a 16" light gray paper strip into an off-centered circle. Pinch a point on the opposite end of the center to make a teardrop. Refer to Teardrop on page 25.

6
Project

What you need to get started:

- General Quilling Tools on pages 10–11

- Foam-tipped chalk applicator

- Fringer

- Light green chalk palette

- Onion holder

- Paper trimmer with cutting and scoring blades

- Periwinkle blue cardstock

- Quilling papers:
  ⅛"-wide brown
  ⅛"-wide leaf green
  ⅛"-wide moss green
  ⅛"-wide white
  ⅜"-wide pale yellow

- Silver embroidery thread

- Teardrop paper punch (optional)

- White text-weight paper

How do I roll quilled crosses?

Here is a beautiful selection of quilled crosses to remember those special religious events. Punched paper, fringing, and chalking are a great combination for creating stunning crosses.

Quilled Crosses

Here's How:

ORNATE CROSS

1. **Quilling Instructions**

   • For the base of the cross, roll ten 8" white paper strips into off-centered circles. Refer to Off-centered Circles Technique on page 29. Pinch four into teardrops. Refer to Teardrop on page 25. Glue the circles and teardrops as shown in 1a.

   • Roll four 2" white paper strips into loose circles. Refer to Loose Circle on page 25. Glue to the ends of the cross as shown in 1a.

   • Roll eight 3" white paper strips into "S" scrolls. Refer to "S" Scroll on page 32. Glue to the cross as shown in 1a.

   • Roll two 3" white paper strips into half circles. Refer to Half Circles on page 25. Glue onto the bottom of the cross as shown in 1a.

   • Fold a 1" white paper strip and roll into a heart scroll. Refer to Heart Scroll on page 32. Glue into the center of the cross.

   • For the top layer, roll five 8" white paper strips into off-centered circles. Pinch into teardrops. Glue them on top of the base as shown in 1b.

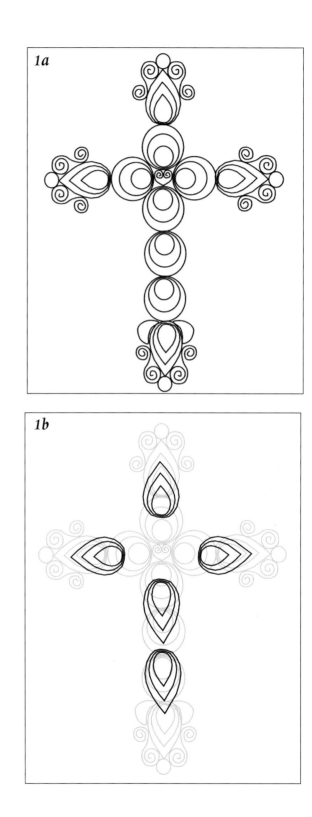

1a

1b

WOODEN CROSS

1. Quilling Instructions

For **Base**:

- Roll eleven 8" brown paper strips into squares. Refer to Square on page 25. Glue together into a cross as shown in 1a.

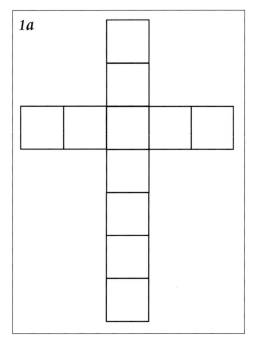

1a

For **Lily**:

- For petals, make 24 teardrops with a hand punch or scissors from white paper. Glue three teardrops together as shown in 1b. Make two sets of three petals for each lily. Roll each set into a cone shape and glue as shown in 1b.

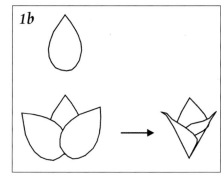

1b

- Glue one cone into the other alternating the tips. Brush light green chalk inside the cone. Make four lilies.

- For lily's center, with ⅜"-wide paper, cut a ½" length pale yellow paper strip. Fringe the entire length. Refer to Fringing Technique on pages 46–47. Cut a slight angle at one end as shown in 1c. Start rolling at the end with the longer fringes and roll a tight circle. Make four centers. Glue centers into lilies.

1c

- For leaves, roll four 4" moss green paper strips into curved marquises for leaves. Refer to Marquise on page 25.

Step 1

2. Glue lilies and leaves to the intersecting corners of the cross.

PALM LEAF CROSS

Note: The size of the cross will depend on the spacing of the prongs.

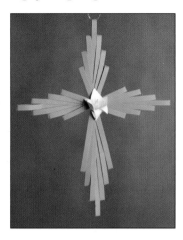

1. **Quilling Instructions**

   For **Cross**:
   - For top and sides, use a full-length leaf green paper strip and the alternate-side combing technique to make the cross as shown in 1a. Refer to Alternate-side Combing Technique on page 64.

   - For bottom, since this portion of the cross is longer, you may need to glue two leaf green paper strips end-to-end. Refer to End-to-end Technique on page 36. Repeat alternating-sides combing technique to make the bottom of the cross as shown in 1a.

   For **Lily**:
   - For petals, make six teardrops with a hand punch or scissors from white paper. Glue three teardrops together as shown in 1b. Make two sets of three petals. Roll each set into a cone shape and glue. Glue one cone into the other alternating the tips. Brush light green chalk inside the cone.

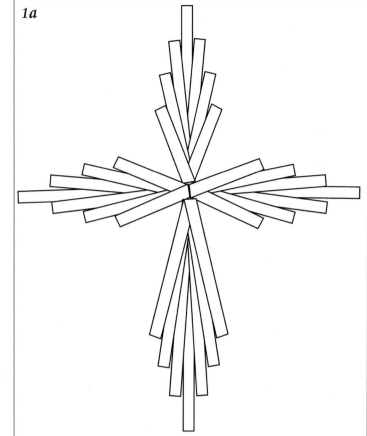

1a

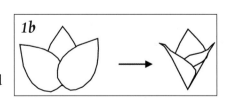

1b

   - For lily's center, use ⅜"-wide paper and ½" length pale yellow paper strip. Fringe the entire length. Cut a slight angle at one end as shown in 1c. Start rolling at the end with the longer fringes and roll into a tight circle. Glue to center of lily.

1c

2. Glue lily at the intersection of the cross.

Step 2

7
Project

What you need to get started:

- General Quilling Tools on pages 10–11

- Fine-tipped felt pens:
  black
  red

- Foam-tipped chalk applicator

- Large crimper

- Marble to help shape pieces

- Pink chalk palette

- Quilling papers:
  ⅛"-wide black
  ⅛"-wide brown
  ⅛"-wide crimson
  ⅛"-wide forest green
  ⅛"-wide pale peach
  ⅛"-wide white
  ¼"-wide black
  ¼"-wide brown
  ¼"-wide white

- White vellum with iridescent specks

How do I quill miniature figurines?

It's surprising how a long paper strip can create such amazing miniatures. I found miniatures to be an addicting technique and a great idea for making figurines and finger puppets for the kids. Be sure to have your fine-tipped tweezers ready to pick up and glue these tiny pieces.

Bride & Groom Cake Topper

Here's How:

Note: Different paper weights and thicknesses may affect how large or wide in diameter your pieces will end up. When the instructions call for a 1/16" paper strip, cut a 1/8"-wide paper in half lengthwise.

1. Review Making Miniatures on pages 67–68 before beginning this project.

2. **Quilling Instructions for Bride**
   - For bun, use 1/16"-wide paper to roll fifteen 1" brown strips into loose scrolls as shown in 2a. Refer to Loose Scroll on page 32.

   - For bangs, use 1/4"-wide paper to cut and round off a 1" and a 1/2" brown paper strips as shown in 2b.

   - For front of head, use 1/8"-wide paper and glue about 48" length or three 16" pale peach strips end-to-end. Refer to End-to-end Technique on page 36. Roll into a 5/8"-diameter tight circle as shown in 2c. Refer to Tight Circle on pages 25–26. Using a marble, evenly shape tight circle into a half dome for face as shown in 2d. Spread glue onto the inside surface and let dry. Using a black and a red pen, draw in the eyes and mouth. Apply some pink chalk on her cheeks.

     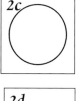

   - For nose, use 1/16"-wide paper to roll a 1/2" pale peach strip into a tight circle and flatten.

   - For back of head, use 1/8"-wide paper, glue three 16" brown strips end-to-end. Roll a 5/8"-diameter tight circle as shown in 2c. Using a marble,

evenly shape into a dome as shown in 2d. Spread glue onto the inside surface and let dry.

   - For veil, cut white vellum into a veil shape as shown in 2e. Run the piece through the crimper so that the crimps are vertical.

     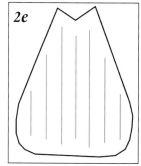

   - For headpiece, use 1/16"-wide paper to roll a 1" white strip into a teardrop. Refer to Teardrop on page 25. Roll two 1" white paper strips into "S" scrolls for headpiece. Refer to "S" Scroll on page 32. Glue one scroll to each side of teardrop as shown in 2f. Use tweezers, to help you shape and handle these pieces.

   - For body, use 1/4"-wide paper and glue about 112" or seven 16" white paper strips end-to-end. Roll into a 1"-diameter tight circle as shown in 2g. Using fingers, shape the tight circle into a cone as shown in 2h. Spread glue onto the inside surface and let dry.

     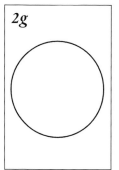

   - For arms, use 1/4"-wide paper to roll two 12" white strips into tight circles as shown in 2i. Using a glue bottle top, shape into a cone as shown in 2j. Slightly

     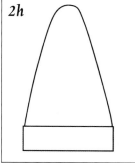

squeeze the cone flat and bend the arm to fit the curvature of the body. Spread glue onto the inside surface and let dry.

- For hands, use ⅛"-wide paper to roll two 8" pale peach strips into tight circles as shown in 2k. Shape 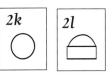 into grape rolls as shown in 2l. Refer to Grape Roll on page 26. Spread glue onto the inside surface and let dry.

3. To form the head, glue the two halves of the head together. Slightly overlap and glue the bangs around the head, covering the seam.

4. Glue the headpiece on top of the bride's head. Using the tweezers, dip each hair curl in some glue and place at the back of the head. Carefully build up the curls of hair to form the bun.

Step 4

5. Glue the hands and arms together. Glue the arms and assembled head onto the body as shown in photograph on page 94. Glue the veil to the back of the head.

6. **Quilling Instructions for Bouquet**

- For flower top, use ¹⁄₁₆"-wide paper to roll five 1" crimson strips into loose scrolls as shown in 6a.

- For flower base, use ¹⁄₁₆"-wide paper to roll six 2" crimson paper strips into teardrops. Glue teardrops together as shown in 6b.

- For leaves, cut three small leaves from ⅛"-wide forest green paper as shown in 6c.

- For handle, roll an 8" forest green strip from ⅛"-wide paper into a tight circle. Shape into a grape roll as shown in 6d.

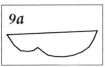

7. To assemble, glue the flower base to the bouquet's handle. Using the tweezers, glue the flower top one by one.

8. Glue the three leaves to the back of bouquet.

9. **Quilling Instructions for Groom**

- For bangs, use ¼"-wide paper, cut and round off a 1" brown paper strip as shown in 9a.

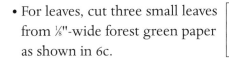

- For front of head, use ⅛"-wide paper and glue about 48" length or three 16" pale peach strips end-to-end. Roll into a ⅝"-diameter tight circle as shown in 9b. Using a marble, evenly shape the tight circle into a half dome for face as shown in 9c. Spread glue onto the inside surface and let dry. Using a black pen, draw in the eyes and the mouth.

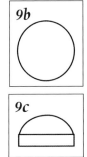

- For nose, use ¹⁄₁₆"-wide paper to roll a ½" pale peach strip into a tight circle and flatten.

- For back of head, use ⅛"-wide paper, glue brown strips about 48" length or three 16" paper strips end-to-end. Roll a ⅝"-diameter tight circle as shown in 9b. Using a marble, evenly shape into a dome as shown in 9c. Spread glue onto the inside surface and let dry.

- For bow tie, use ¹⁄₁₆"-wide paper to roll two 2" black strips into triangles. Refer to Triangle on page 25. Use tweezers to help you shape and handle these pieces. Use ¼"-wide white paper,

cut a 1" strip into the
shape of a tuxedo shirt as
shown in 9d. Using a
black pen, make several
dots in a vertical line for
buttons. From ¼"-wide
paper, cut two 1" black
strips into the shape of a
tuxedo lapel as shown in 9d.

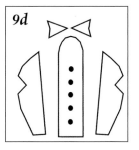

- For body, use ¼"-wide paper, glue black strips
  about 64" length or four 16" end-to-end. Roll
  into a ¾"-diameter tight circle as shown in 9e.
  Using your fingers, shape the tight circle into a
  cone as shown in 9f. Spread glue onto the
  inside surface and let dry.

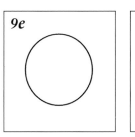

- For arms, use ⅛"-wide
  paper to roll two 12" black
  strips into tight circles as
  shown in 9g. Using the glue
  bottle top, help shape the
  piece into a cone as shown in 9h.
  Slightly squeeze the cone flat and bend the
  arm to fit the curvature of the body. Spread
  glue onto the inside surface and let dry.

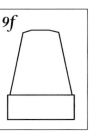

- For hands, use ⅛"-wide to
  roll two 8" pale peach strips
  paper into tight circles as
  shown in 9i. Shape into
  grape rolls as shown in 9j.
  Spread glue onto the inside
  surface and let dry.

- For leg, use ¼"-wide paper
  to roll six 16" black strips
  into tight circles as shown
  in 9k. Glue three tight

circles on top of each other to form one leg
as shown in 9l. Repeat for the remaining tight
circles.

- For shoes, use ⅛"-wide paper to roll
  two 8" black strips into teardrops as
  shown in 9m.

10. To form the head, glue the two
    halves of the head together. Slightly
    overlap and glue the bangs around the head,
    covering the seam.

11. To make the tuxedo, glue the rounded end of
    the shirt to the top of the body. Glue the two
    lapel pieces at an angle, slightly overlapping at
    the "waist." Glue the bow tie pieces to the shirt.

Step 11

12. Glue the shoes to the leg pieces and glue legs
    into body. Check to see that he can stand up on
    his own. Glue the hands to the arms. Glue the
    arms and head to the body.

13. **Quilling Instructions for Boutonniere**
    - For flower, use ¹⁄₁₆"-wide paper to roll
      a 1" crimson strip into a loose scroll
      as shown in 13a.

    - For stem, use ¹⁄₁₆"- wide paper to roll a
      1" forest green strip into a cone roll as
      shown in 13a.

    - Glue the flower to the stem.

14. Glue the boutonniere to his lapel as shown in
    photograph on page 94.

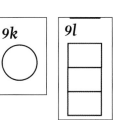

8
Project

What you need to get started:

- General Quilling Tools on pages 10–11

- ⅛"-wide quilling papers:
  beige
  forest green
  pumpkin

- Brown chalk palette

- Corkboard

- Foam-tipped chalk applicator

- Night-light with shade

- Onion holder
  (optional)

How can I illuminate quilled artwork?

Growing up in an Asian culture, I've always loved looking at oriental art. The gallery shows a grouping of quilled oriental flowers that was inspired by Chinese paintings. Here is a simple bamboo project that, when illuminated, will bring a feeling of the orient into your home.

Oriental Bamboo Night-light

Here's How:

Note: These bamboo leaves can be made looping continuous center loops by hand, with either the husking technique or the one-side combing technique.

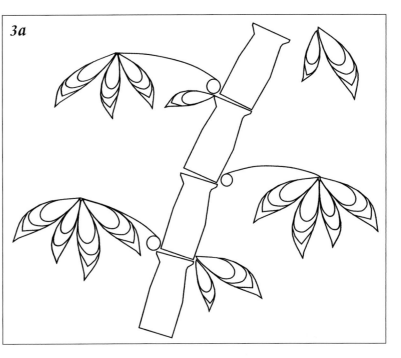

3a

1. Braid three pumpkin paper strips. Refer to Braiding Technique on page 58. Glue onto the top and bottom of the night-light.

2. Add chalk on the braided paper strips and onto the lampshade.

3. **Quilling Instructions**

   For **Bamboo Stem**:
   • Roll four 16" beige paper strips into rectangles. Refer to Rectangle on page 25. At one end, pinch and curve the two points inward as shown in 3a. Glue the bamboo pieces together along short sides. Add brown chalk on top of the quilling where the pieces are glued at the bamboo joints.

Step 3

   For **Branches**:
   • Roll half of a 3" beige paper strip into a tight circle, leaving the other end straight. Refer to Tight Circle on pages 25–26. Make three branches.

For **Leaves**:
• Using the Wheatear Looping Technique on page 55 or the Husking Technique on page 51, make random sized leaves with forest green paper strips.

Step 4

4. Glue the leaves in groups. Glue onto branches.

5. Glue the bamboo stem at an angle on the night-light shade.

6. Glue the branches at the joints of the bamboo. *Note: Use the needle tool or fine-tipped glue bottle to add small drops of glue behind the quilled pieces so that they lay flat against the shade.*

Section 4: *Gallery*

Alli Bartkowski (author)

This high school senior portrait frame, featured at right, was custom quilled for a very talented violinist. The violin is pieced together with basic quilled shapes and completed with music notes and classical sheet music. The colors of the flowers represent the colors of the university that the graduate selected.

The oriental flower series on page 101 was inspired by traditional oriental paintings where seasons are represented by a different flower. The plum blossoms (spring), lotus flower (summer), chrysanthemums (fall), and bamboo (winter) were created with similar techniques described in this book.

Examples of Alli's scrapbook page designs are on pages 30, 84, and 103. They are precious and fleeting moments that are enhanced with some adorable quilled pieces from Alli's "Baby Theme" and "Just for Little Girls" quilling kits.

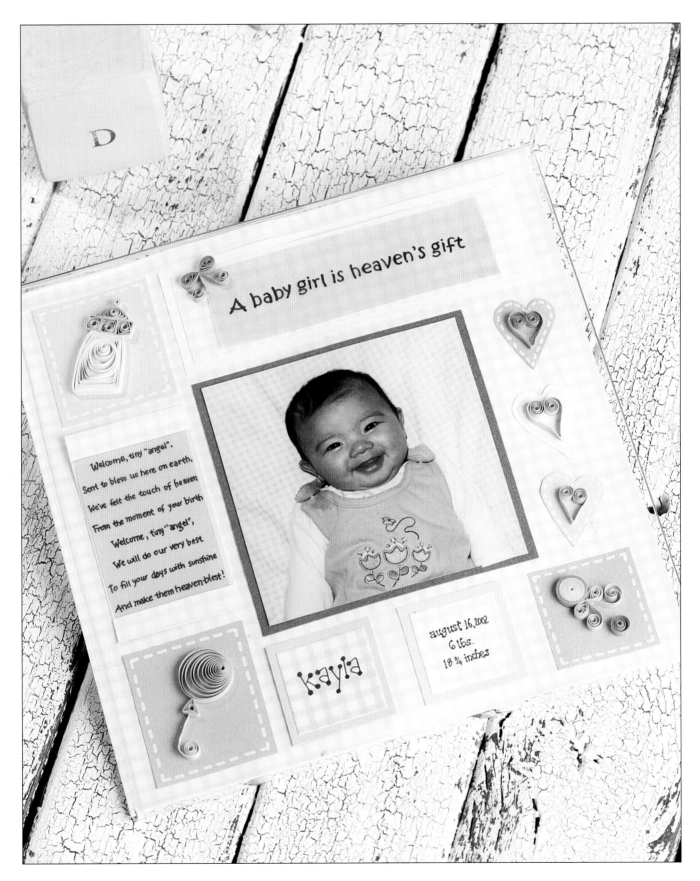

A baby girl is heaven's gift

Welcome, tiny "angel",
Sent to bless us here on earth,
We've felt the touch of heaven
From the moment of your birth.
Welcome, tiny "angel",
We will do our very best
To fill your days with sunshine
And make them heaven-blest!

Kayla

august 16, 2002
6 lbs.
18 ¾ inches

Linda Grisham

Linda first tried quilling during its last popularity in the 1970s. Now, after years of scrapbooking and stamping, she has developed her own style of quilling called, "SparQuilling Ink." She enjoys combining quilling with stamping, punching, dry embossing, pergamano, and other paper art techniques. Her quilled cards featured on pages 104–105 are beautifully embellished with glitter, beads, fibers, and other materials to create an elegant look to her designs.

Linda is a member of the North American Quilling Guild and currently teaches quilling in the San Diego, California, area. Her Web site, www.spar-quillingink.com, showcases her talent in quilling cards, scrapbook pages, and frames. Aside from throwing quilling parties and creating new card designs, Linda is certified in Art Clay Silver and PMC.

Sherry Rodehaver

Sherry began her quilling adventure in 1972 when she taught herself how to quill and design miniatures. Over the years, her quilled miniatures have become famous at the Yankee Peddler Festival in Canal Fulton, Ohio, where she has exhibited her artwork for 30 years now. Her clients consider her quilled miniatures to be collectibles and she has over 75 miniature designs to date. Her pieces are highly detailed and are composed of the most intricate and minute bits of quilled paper.

Sherry's "Bakery," at right, is a stunning example of her unique and talented style in quilling. Sherry first wrote out the bakery sign, listing all of her favorite baked goods. Then she set out to create each scrumptious goodie on the sign. "It was challenging," she laughs, "if I was to do another one, I would make the baked goods first, then the sign!" Sherry has shown through her quilling that nothing is impossible but more a question of "how can it be accomplished?"

She is a proud member of the North American Quilling Guild and is an accredited member of the English Quilling Guild. She is most intrigued by anything miniature and the history of paper crafts. She adds, "Paper is my instrument of my expression. I hope to inspire future generations to keep the valued art of quilling alive and well." Her whimsical miniature animals are featured on pages 100, 108, and 112.

Fredricka Whitman

Fredricka has been quilling since 1990 and is a member of the North American Quilling Guild. Her inspiration for this beautiful three-dimensional hummingbird was from a picture on a cover of a magazine. The entire piece took over 120 hours to complete, with the hummingbird alone taking half the time. This amazing piece won first place and the Peoples Choice Award at the 2004 NAQG Annual Meeting in Plymouth, Massachusetts. Her favorite use for quilling is cross-stitching verses and embellishing them with quilled and punched flowers.

About the Author

Allison (Alli) Bartkowski has a BS in Mechanical Engineering and a MS in Manufacturing Engineer and Product Design. After college, she worked on designing printers at a well-known copier company where she studied the "science of removing the curl from paper." In 2002, after the birth of her second daughter, she made the decision to become a full-time stay-at-home mom. At the same time, her husband had the brilliant idea of turning her favorite hobbies, quilling and scrapbooking, into an online business, "Quilled Creations." Alli started creating quilling designs for her scrapbooks, hence, her own line of quilling kits was born. She finds her new career (now, ironically, teaching the "art of curling paper") relaxing and very rewarding.

Because of her engineering background and her interest in designing products, she felt the need to design "easier to use" and reliable quilling tools. Today, her tools and kits are helping beginners around the world learn this wonderful art.

"Quilled Creations," www.quilledcreations.com, is now an internationally known company and her high quality products and kits are sold in craft and scrapbooking stores around the world. Alli's kits and tools were featured on national television and are sold in craft catalogs throughout the world.

Alli is a member of the Craft and Hobby Association and North American Quilling Guild. The quilled masterpieces made by guild members shown in the Gallery, prove that you can create almost anything with simple strips of papers.

Alli lives in Rochester, New York, with her husband Dave and their two daughters, Rachel and Kayla.

Dedication

To my daughters, Rachel and Kayla—your beautiful smiles bring pure joy to my heart.

Acknowledgments

This book exists through the support and inspiration from many friends and family members. For all of your contributions, my deepest thank-you.

To the gallery artists and NAQG members, for sharing your designs and creative talent. To Karmen Quinney and Chapelle, Ltd., for this wonderful opportunity. To Ana Tooker, you were there when it all began. To Tina Arcoraci, for your enthusiasm and amazing attention to details. To my sister, Aimee Repp, for the adorable photograph of your son and for many "sanity-check" phone calls. To my aunt, Una Shih, for your help and generosity in too many ways to count. To my parents, for your unconditional love and guidance throughout my life. I'm eternally grateful for having your help with watching the girls and for your digital photography expertise. To my loving husband, Dave, thank-you for being an incredible "Mr. Mom" while putting this book together. Your wisdom, encouragement, and patience are what I love about you.

PHOTOGRAPHY
Alli Bartkowski: 8–21, 25–27, 29–30 (ur), 32–34, 36–37, 39–40, 42–43, 46–49, 51–52, 54–56, 58–60, 62, 64–65, 67–68, 70–71, 75 (ur), 76 (ll, ur), 77, 79, 83, 85, 87, 89, 91–93, 97, 99
Don Cole: 106–107, 109

Zac Williams, Chapelle Ltd.: 1–4, 6–7, 20, 22–24, 28, 30 (ur), 31, 35, 38, 41, 44–45, 50, 53, 57, 61, 63, 66, 69, 72–74, 75 (ul, lr), 76 (lr), 78, 81, 84, 86, 90, 93–94, 98, 100–105, 108, 112

Metric Equivalency Chart

mm-millimeters   cm-centimeters
inches to millimeters and centimeters

inches	mm	cm	inches	cm	inches	cm
⅛	3	0.3	9	22.9	30	76.2
¼	6	0.6	10	25.4	31	78.7
½	13	1.3	12	30.5	33	83.8
⅝	16	1.6	13	33.0	34	86.4
¾	19	1.9	14	35.6	35	88.9
⅞	22	2.2	15	38.1	36	91.4
1	25	2.5	16	40.6	37	94.0
1¼	32	3.2	17	43.2	38	96.5
1½	38	3.8	18	45.7	39	99.1
1¾	44	4.4	19	48.3	40	101.6
2	51	5.1	20	50.8	41	104.1
2½	64	6.4	21	53.3	42	106.7
3	76	7.6	22	55.9	43	109.2
3½	89	8.9	23	58.4	44	111.8
4	102	10.2	24	61.0	45	114.3
4½	114	11.4	25	63.5	46	116.8
5	127	12.7	26	66.0	47	119.4
6	152	15.2	27	68.6	48	121.9
7	178	17.8	28	71.1	49	124.5
8	203	20.3	29	73.7	50	127.0

Index

DATE DUE

APR 0 7			
APR 2 9			
APR 2 0			
JUN 0 3			
OCT 0 2			
GAYLORD			PRINTED IN U.S.A.